Beyond the Beat

Your guide for before and after heart surgery or a heart attack for emotional resilience.

SALLIE CRAWLEY

ISBN: 978-1-7399806-2-7

Contents

1Disclaimer 5

Introduction 7

You Are Not Alone 11

- Ted Baker, Hull, England, UK 11
- Herbert Blair, Central Pennsylvania, USA 12
- Jacki Cloud, NW Michigan, USA 20
- Denise Earley, Southampton, England UK 29
- Don Helm, Delaware, USA 30
- Kimberley Ann Milley (Morgan), Newfoundland & Labrador, CA 34
- Terri Picton-Clark (Dancing Nana), Leicestershire, England UK 39
- Jackie Smith, Whittlesey, Cambridgeshire, England UK 43
- Brett White, Missouri, USA 48
- David Wood, England UK 51

The Journey: Before and After Your Open-Heart Surgery 53

- Preparing for Liftoff: Pre-Surgery 54
- Recovery Runway: Post-Surgery 55
- Landing Strip: Journeying at Home 56

It's ALL about You! 58
Let's go do this together! 61
An Interesting Year - Oh My Life! 62
Share your experience 68
Life After Your Heart Event 69
Find a buddy who's walked your path 71
Making It Through the Early Days 72
Your contact list 75
It's good to talk 76
Be kind to yourself 77
Emotional awareness 77
Be in the now 79
The spiral of twelve 80
Use your recovery time 80
Friends and family 81
Set mini-missions for the day 82
Find the treasure 82
Find a purpose 83
Empower Your Life 84
Journaling 85
Is Anxiety Good or Bad? 94
Breathe 95
Mind-body connection 95
Reduce stimulants 96
Befriend your heartbeat 97

- Who are you talking to and what are you saying? ... 98
- Lavender ... 98
- Gratitude graffiti ... 99
- Move your body ... 99
- Time to unwind ... 100
- Nurture your green spirit ... 101
- Take a mental holiday ... 102
- Embrace the power of "no" ... 103

Changing How You Feel About Pain ... 104

- Four square breathing ... 106
- Distract yourself ... 106
- Soak in a warm bath or take a shower ... 107
- Laugh your heart out (not literally!) ... 108
- Channel your inner artist ... 108
- What are you saying about your pain? ... 109
- Essential oils ... 110
- Let it go … A pain & discomfort reframe ... 111
- Visualise your victory lap ... 113
- Journaling for chronic pain ... 113

Restoring Your Sleep ... 116

- Download my sleep easy checklist ... 127

Love, Sex, and Intimacy ... 128

- How do you feel about sex are you ready? ... 130
- Open communication ... 130
- Go slow ... 131

Educate yourself 131
Celebrate your body 131
Seek professional guidance 131
Get connected with other single people 131
Shadows of the Heart - Cardiophobia 132
Understanding the normalcy of sensations 135
Accurate information 135
Mindful breathing 135
Stay in the now, this MOMENT 135
Progressive muscle relaxation (PMR) 136
Challenge negative thoughts 137
Incorporate relaxing activities 138
Connect with other hearties 139
Open communication 139
Shadows of the Heart - Pumphead 141
Mental gymnastics 143
Physical exercise 143
Mindful meditation 143
Adequate sleep 144
Balanced nutrition 144
Social engagement 144
It's Time to Say 'Until Next Time' 146
About The Author 148
Other Books on Amazon 149

Disclaimer

The information contained within this book is for general information purpose only. It is not official health advice and is not intended to be used as such.

Any action you take upon the information you find in this book is strictly at your own risk.

Any material or information in this book is not medical or therapeutic and is not intended to diagnose, treat, cure or prevent any medical condition or disease.

If you have any questions pertaining to specific health concerns or you think you may be suffering from a medical condition, you should consult a medical professional immediately.

You should also consult a medical professional before making any changes to your normal lifestyle habits.

Limitation of warranties
The medical information in this book is provided 'as is' without any representations or warranties, express or implied. This book makes no representations or warranties in relation to the medical information contained within it.

Professional assistance

You must not rely on the information in this book as an alternative to medical advice from your doctor or other professional healthcare provider.

If you have concerns about any medical matter, your physical or mental health, you should consult your doctor or other professional healthcare provider immediately.

Information included in this book is not intended to replace conventional medicine, it is complementary.

If you think you may be suffering from any medical condition you should seek immediate medical attention.

You should never delay seeking medical advice, disregard medical advice, or discontinue medical treatment because of the information in this book.

Results may vary from person to person. The content of these pages has been developed to assist you and give no guarantee; you yourself can be the only person that can provide a guarantee for your own success.

Liability

Nothing in this medical disclaimer will limit any of our liabilities in any way that is not permitted under applicable law, or exclude any of our liabilities that may not be excluded under applicable law.

By using the information in this book, you hereby consent to my disclaimer and agree to its terms.

Introduction

I'm so glad you have chosen to join me, welcome great to meet you, please get yourself comfortable. Like you, I have experienced events in my life that have turned it upside down.

In 2016, and not for the first time, my life had become almost unrecognisable in a matter of 6 months. It all started with a freak accident. It was February and I was on a mission of wellbeing. It was in the middle of my regular martial arts class that I ruptured my Achilles tendon. It was during my recovery 4 weeks later that I had a heart attack. Then 8 weeks after that, I had a diagnosis of breast cancer. All this as well as being a single mum to an amazing teenage girl.

Whilst I can only imagine what it would be like after open heart surgery, stepping out of that hospital post-heart attack was like breaking free from a cocoon. Yeah, there was freedom, but it came wrapped in this weird fragility I'd never known. My heart beats? Sounded like a drum solo, a constant reminder of the battle I'd fought and, thank heavens, won. But fear stuck to me like glue. Every little twinge, each flutter, had me in a panic. The trauma? Oh, it wasn't just physical; it was etched into my very soul, beneath that not-so-stylish hospital gown I'd swapped for my comfy home clothes.

Fatigue – it clung to me like a cloak made of lead. Simple tasks? Left me gasping for air. Exercise, my old pal, turned into this intimidating mountain to climb. And food? Well, it went from being a source of joy to navigating a minefield of "good" and "bad." Every choice felt like life and death – drama much?

They talked about the "new normal" like it was just around the corner. But honestly, it felt like a distant mirage, shimmering in the desert of my recovery. Sleep? Oh, it used to be a sweet escape. Now, it was a battlefield. My body, on high alert, refused to give in. Nights became a series of phantom pains and runaway thoughts, each dawn bringing a bone-deep exhaustion. Irritability? That flared up like a firework show – my system, overloaded with fear and anxiety, just short-circuited.

Yet, amid of all that chaos, a tiny spark of determination flickered. This so-called "new normal," as scary as it seemed, I wasn't going to be ruled by fear. No way. It was going to be a journey – one wobbly step at a time, as I slowly took back my life, beat by hesitant beat. Because, let me tell you, reclaiming your life! It's like rewriting your own story, one where you get to be a resilient hero. And that, my friend, is a journey worth taking.

If any of that sounds familiar then this book is for you. I want to join you in your journey, walking beside you step by step. Later in the book I will share with you in detail what I needed to help me become the resilient hero.

I am on a mission in life to reassure everyone it is not one size fits all. We are all unique, not one person has the identical fingerprints as you, so why would the same technique or process work for everyone.

In this book you will read about some ideas, activities and downloads for you to try out, just have a go – some may be a bit meh to you, and yet others may be life improving. Think of it as a pick and mix, choose only those that you like. You may find you want to come back to some that didn't float your boat at a later date of your recovery.

I do try hard to make life simple and be down with the kids, so where there is a download or URL, I have also included a QR code. You are then able to scan this on your phone and it will take you directly to the links so you have the choice of how to access them.

The one constant thing in life is change. Yet, that doesn't mean you get used to it or can fully embrace it immediately. With time you can be flexible in your thoughts, feelings and behaviours and you will adapt that really counts for your recovery. Since most of us go through changes in our lives, I thought I would share with you briefly what I found helped me the most.

These are my six pillars of emotional rehabilitation when dealing with big changes in your life and developing your 'new normal'.

1. Acceptance of the situation, myself, my body, what was and what is now including my limitations. My favourite saying was 'it is, what it is'!

2. Energy to fuel my recovery both physically and emotionally. It gave me the motivation and drive to want more each and every day. No more I'll do it tomorrow as it may never come.

3. Hope as I no longer wanted the 'why me' feeling. Having hope helped me to connect with people. It helped me look forward. I began to see new situations and circumstances more positively. I was able to start looking outside myself. Rather than dwelling inside on my thoughts and feelings.

4. Purpose in my life. I was so energised from the moment I realised I had a vision and I was driven to achieve it. My purpose was to help people like me. Those who felt overwhelmed by the impact of their life and the changes that had happened.

5. Confidence was key to getting my life back. I was scared and felt lost. By gaining confidence I was able to push right outside

my comfort zone. I have even walked on hot coals since, very life-affirming.

6. Direction is a very important state of mind. Knowing where to start and what I needed to do to achieve to get where I wanted. I had been through a stressful physical and emotional period. I needed to focus on the next steps for wellness. I knew what I wanted and like when you're on a journey I needed a map or a Satnav to help me find my way.

So, let's turn the pages as we take our journey together. It's not just about surviving; I want to help you thrive and feel good now. To take control of your life. I have chosen to become a heart attack warrior!

I believe I'm lucky. My heart attack is one of my life experiences. I choose to see it as a great opportunity to focus on the things that really matter, to live and love life.

My mission is to be of service to help as many people as possible with their emotional and practical recovery and this means you. I am here to help you gain control and power over your life after a cardiac event.

You Are Not Alone

"One day you will tell your story of how you overcame what you went through and it will be someone else's survival guide." Brene Brown

In the beginning, I felt okay about having a heart attack although it didn't seem real or that serious at first. After a few days, the enormity began to set it as I had more time to think about what happened. I started to feel alone, I had questions but no one to ask and no one to talk to that knew how I felt. Most importantly there was no one to tell me it was going to be alright.

This chapter is a collection of stories from survivors and thrivers. It is their own words describing their event and the heart journey. My hope is that you will take comfort from their words. That you will feel inspired and believe that you can do this because if they did then you sure as hell can too.

Ted Baker, Hull, England, UK

In 2001 had I had a massive Heart Attack. I was dead for 20 minutes but I was brought back to life. I was in Hull Royal Infirmary for 6 days and then was back at work 12 months later.

It was in 2016 that I failed my HGV medical on cardiac stress test. I had an angiogram and it found that I had 3 arteries 100% blocked and another with a 75% blockage. Later in July 2017 I had triple bypass as they couldn't do the 4th smaller blockage.

I was in the Castle Hill Hospital for 4 days and then back at work in 11 weeks as an HGV mechanic. My recovery was good as I had the determination to get better and that is the key. After my surgery, the driving force to recover and get well again to enjoy life, was my six Grandchildren and to enjoy my life.

Ninety percent of recovery is all about mental attitude, as an ex-soldier you learn to adapt and overcome. You can sit in a chair and do nothing and be saying woe is me or get off your backside and do cardio rehab, eat healthy and do plenty of walking and it will make a vast difference to your mental health and wellbeing.

I chose to take retirement in 2018 but I got bored so I retrained and took my HGV class1 driving test which I passed. I now travel around the UK carrying abnormal loads at the young age of 70. I will be 71 in July 24 and I am enjoying life. I love walking and playing games with my grandchildren. I certainly don't feel my age either.

The operation was the best thing that happened to me. I feel very well, have no angina and I am enjoying life. Have my HGV medical every year and get my licence back each time. Mental attitude is the key to getting well. Enjoy life and make the most of it. I hope everyone takes heart from this little story.

Herbert Blair, Central Pennsylvania, USA

A little background first. My wife and I have been married over 50 years now. It was 3 years ago when my cardiac event happened. I was 71 years old and had retired a little over a year before in 2020 just before the COVID outbreak. My wife has had many health problems, not of her own doing, and I was always in the "caregiver" position. My health had always been much better than most people my age.

During the "COVID lockdown" my wife and I tried to find places where we could avoid human contact. We were walking on the large grounds of a military museum in a nearby town. I started to feel like

I had the wind knocked out of me, becoming very tired and feeling like my face was numb and someone was sticking pins into it. I had never felt that way before. I couldn't keep up with my wife and finally asked her to slow down and it was a real chore to make it back to the car. After I sat down, I felt a little better but not great. I drove to a grocery store on the way home and was able to make my purchase and get home but still felt off. My wife was very concerned and thought we should go to the hospital emergency room but I said no, I'd see a doctor the next day since it was late afternoon. It probably wasn't the wisest decision.

The next morning, I ended up in the cardiologist office and related the events from the previous day and told him I had no idea what caused me to feel that way. The doctor and his assistant said they were 99 percent sure that they did. An hour later, I was on my back in the hospital having a heart catheterization. Because of the COVID rules, my wife couldn't go into the hospital and had to wait outside. The doctor called my wife and told her it was bad, very bad. I had 6 major blockages, from 80 percent up to 99 percent for most of them, and I needed to have a multiple heart bypass operation. He was able to let my wife in to see me for about 10 minutes, with masking, before I was taken by ambulance to a major medical/research hospital 2 hours away.

Until I got there, we didn't know if they'd let my wife in to see me because of the COVID restrictions. My wife had to stay behind, at home, until the next morning, until we got clearance from the hospital to let her visit, and ONLY her, during the time I was there. I was told that I would have to have triple bypass surgery (CABG3) and since it was the wee hours of Friday morning when I arrived, the surgery would probably be Monday morning unless things got even worse. I spent the weekend undergoing all sorts of questions, and tests, and vein mapping. They put me on medication that would lower my blood pressure and also dilate my blood vessels. They selected the best veins from my leg to be "harvested" that they would use for my bypass repair. They said they were doing all this so they didn't have any surprises when they went in on Monday. I found out, after my asking, that the average life expectancy of a bypass repair was 10 years but I was not to dwell on that information. My job was to do everything possible to heal and live a healthy life so I could extend that time after my procedure. Their job was to do their best to repair me. Coming from an engineering background, it still concerns me, but like they said, live and eat healthy.

On Monday morning, they prepped me for surgery. I convinced my wife to go back home so she could get her second COVID shot the next morning to protect her as much as possible due to her own pulmonary health issues. She wasn't allowed to stay in the hospital during my operation. She really didn't want to leave me but I told her that if I made it through the operation, I'd see her the next day, and if I didn't, I wanted her to be okay with her health. She reluctantly left after kissing me, each of us knowing it may be the last time we'd see each other on this side of heaven. I made sure EVERYONE knew my wife's cellphone number so they could call her and assure her that I made it through surgery alive. They took me down to the operating room and she stayed with me until she wasn't allowed any further. Just before she left, we both gave each other our special signal of assurance. Whenever she was taken to surgery, we each looked at each other and cupped one of our hands to remind each other that God held her, or me, in the hollow of His hand. It had always been for her. Now it was my turn.

They wheeled me into the operating room. It was so cold and I was shivering but was told that after a short while they would put warm towels on me where they could to make me warmer. Never having an operation before, all these people and the equipment was a bit overwhelming. I asked "Is this all for me?", and they said "yes, there are multiple teams that will be working on you at the same time. Some will be harvesting your veins, some anaesthesia, surgeons for your heart, people monitoring your vital signs, etcetera. We're going to take good care of you". But my Scottish ancestry kicked in and I said out loud "I can only imagine what this is going to cost". They looked at me, half laughing, and said "THIS is what you're worried about?" As it turned out, I never got a bill. Thank God, it was covered.

I checked and was told everything had been paid. That was one worry gone.

While lying on the operating table being prepped, I had the most intense conversation with God that I have ever had. Only He and I know the full details, but I had peace that everything would be all right. My biggest concern was being around to continue to be with my wife and not make her a widow nor sad. Well, my surgery was a bit delayed, as sometimes happens, and my wife hadn't heard anything by the time she made it home, two hours away. Then she got a call. The nurse on the other end said she was calling from the operating room. My wife apparently said "Oh no!" The nurse hearing that said "No, everything is okay. Your husband wanted to make sure someone called you and let you know he was okay. He's still under anaesthesia but the operation went well and he'll be going into recovery soon.

Late on Monday, in Recovery, I started to wake up. I had almost a dozen tubes, and wires coming out of my chest and abdomen. I was welcomed back to the world by a nurse and asked how I felt. I was told I probably would not remember much from that day and that was normal, but I seem to remember more than I was expected too though. They packed a lot of pain medicine into my chest, so I would be somewhat pain free for about 12 hours, and then the fun begins. I do recall that I asked for a Coca-Cola. I didn't immediately get solid food until the next day. They had me in this post-recovery area for a day or so. There were a few tubes in me that had to be removed before I was moved to a private room in the cardiac care unit.

It was in the oldest part of the hospital, so it was smaller, and not big enough for anyone else in another bed except me and the equipment around me. Honestly, I wouldn't have wanted another patient in the room. I just wanted to get well enough to go home and recover. I definitely didn't want a "chatty" person in a bed next to me. It was all I could do to concentrate on me. Normally, I expected to be in the hospital for 4 or 5 days. For me, counting the initial 3 days until the day of surgery, I was there an additional 14 days, a total of 17 days, which while they claimed it sometimes happens, was frustrating for me. Over that period of time, there was, of course, bloodwork every day, chest x-rays, examinations, visits by doctors and nurses, and questions. I seemed to be healing well, but they were concerned that I hadn't had, not to be indelicate, but my first post-op bowel movement. It may sound trivial but it concerned me also. Now, I am as regular as Old Faithful (a geyser in one of our national parks that erupts like clockwork), as they say here in America. It took six days. I felt the need, but I was scared that if I pushed at all, the strain of it would "blow out" the newly installed bypasses around my heart. When a nurse suggested I "push" hard, I told her my concerns. She had one of the doctors come in and explain that when I left the operating room, their bypasses were as strong as they would ever be, and that I wouldn't cause harm to myself. After that, my body started to work again. This is an example of the type of concern that I'm sure many people have. If I had asked more questions things would have worked faster. One question that I did ask was "did you clear all my blockages" Their answer was "We accomplished everything we intended to do to maximize your blood flow". I knew what they meant.

During this hospital stay, they needed to get my medication adjusted so my heart worked well. I had bouts of A-fib, irregular heart rhythms, and problems that I had never had before. They told me that it was normal until they zeroed in on the right medications and dosage. It seemed to me that I would never be "normal" again. I asked them "Is this what the rest of my life is going to be like?" I felt I was worse off than before the operation and was really depressed. I needed to get up and walk around the unit but when things would go crazy with my rhythms and blood pressure, it was immediately back to my bed so nothing horrible happened. Finally, my heart started to calm down, trigger properly, and my med changes slowed dramatically. It seemed like they were narrowing down on what I needed. I started walking in the hallways of the unit and would check the various monitor displays to see what my blood pressure and rhythms were doing and adjusted my walking to keep things within the limits. I began to get stronger and more confident.

One of the biggest problems for me was trying to sleep the way I wanted. I am a side sleeper so that was totally out of the question. It wasn't good for healing and with the pain, it didn't work. I took the pain medication as I needed but I couldn't play "tough guy" because if the pain got ahead of me, it took a while to get it back to comfortable levels.

I was told pre-operation that I would probably become very emotional for a while after the operation. My wife was there visiting and we were talking with my sister on the phone. I became overwhelmingly sad, felt everyone hated me, and had a tremendous meltdown, crying and wailing very loudly. It was horrible. Now, none of what I felt was true, but it seemed real and terrifying at the time. I will say, however, that since my CABG3, even after three years, I feel things much more deeply, and feel I see things so much more clearly that before. I wasn't heartless before (yes, pun intended) but I feel things so much more deeply now.

The food in the hospital actually was very appealing but I didn't have a big appetite. I felt badly for the dietitians that brought me my meals. They looked so good but I couldn't eat a lot of it. I lost 17 pounds while in the hospital.

Finally, the day came and I was discharged, with temporary restrictions. No driving for 4 weeks, no lifting more than 10 pounds for 6 weeks, no lifting more than 20 pounds for the next 6 weeks after that. I was to have a follow-up visit with the cardiac doctors a week or two later. I was put on Coumadin for 3 months to lessen the chance of blood clots, with regular blood tests, and contact by phone with the anticoagulation team two hours away from my home.

I also had to get used to my "new" body. After the doctors saw you open, make necessary repairs, push your chest back together, wire and sew it shut, it doesn't exactly look like it did coming from the factory. The two little incisions in my leg were no big deal, but that one down the center of my chest took some getting used to. My wife was once told by a doctor, after all her operations that her scars were evidence of "victories won". I had to start thinking of my scar that way. It did bother me for a long while. I initially had a lot of keloid scarring but as time has gone on, a lot of the keloid scarring has turned to just a line. I was told by my cardiologist that the keloid stuff could be removed by a cosmetic surgeon, but I've made peace with it and don't want to be vain about it. Like it was said – Victory Won. I don't mind going topless (shirtless) at the beach now. I even found a shirt at a store that said "Scars are tattoos with better stories" but not for wearing at the beach.

After my surgery, I was worried about all sorts of things. Could I do this? Should I do that? Why can't I do what I did before? Since I was always the "caregiver" and the person who could do anything in the eyes of my family, they were all in shock, as I was, that I had this happen. I never knew they thought of me as a kind of Superman. They were so worried that they almost lost me that they all went into super protective mode. My wife, understandably, was worried when I did anything that might stress my body or soul. I was told that there were two factors that caused my coronary artery disease. First, my dad died at 70, my grandparents (my dad's parents) died at 73 and 74. All of heart attacks. Second factor was high stress. Diet nor weight were really a factor in it, heredity and stress were. I was told that if I didn't get a handle on my stress, that I would be back there sooner than later. So, everyone wanted to treat me like some kind of fragile human being.

I was given cookbooks on healthy eating, a large container of mixed nuts, given suggestions on what I could do to live healthier. All good things but I also needed to live a normal life and have people understand that I too cared about me. Yes, we all had a big scare but I needed to convince myself that I could do most things, safely, again. My triple bypass was on March 1, 2021. We were still in COVID restriction mode so my cardiac rehabilitation at our local hospital wasn't going to happen just then. Later, in the early summer, my cardiologist set me up with cardiac rehab so I could get past my concerns about my capabilities. Just after I completed that, we went on vacation to the beach and also made a day trip down to the Outer

Banks of North Carolina. There is a large state park there, with huge sand dunes. We all walked up the difficult side of the dunes to the top and flew kites up there. Getting up there was the strenuous part but I actually did well and it really boosted my confidence that I was actually getting myself back.

Later in the year, as winter, and snow, came. I also had to modify my routine. I am no longer shoveling or at least lifting snow, but I can still clear it, with modifications. I now have a battery powered snow blower, a snow thrower, and can clear snow with a shovel as long as I do it slowly and just push it. In the spring of the following year, we vacationed at another beach and I went to a lighthouse that I have previously climbed. This was my next big test. I climbed all 199 steps to its top. My oldest son told me he was watching me the whole time but even he felt I did well. I needed to prove to myself that I could still do it. It meant a lot to me.

In the three years since my CABG3, I have become stronger, more confident, and health smart. I've changed some my bad eating habits and I am still working on getting better at that, even though it wasn't a major factor in my coronary artery disease. I have cut my cholesterol in half. I try to exercise with my wife at a local gym three times a week and really enjoy the rowing machine the most out of the different machines I use. My cardiologist said that the rowing machine is the best overall form of exercise he would recommend since it works so much of your body as well as good cardio.

Three years ago, I was really concerned that I might die, even though my health had been better than normal, in my eyes. I know I'm not the same as I was then. I'm not as strong physically. It has taken a toll going through this, but I am so grateful for what I've learned since then and the people who have cared for and about me. I think the biggest asset I had, besides God Himself, was a mind determined to get through this and do my best to get on the other side of the worst day in my life. It's do-able if you want it bad enough.

Jacki Cloud, NW Michigan, USA

Hi I'm Jacki, I'm a wife, Mom, Gramma, retired corrections officer, part time pickup shopper. I'm a CABGX3 survivor, never thought I'd say that, but here I am. My mother had a new valve and CABGX5 when she was 75, but she had multiple health issues. Why would I need surgery at 67? My family generally dies of heart disease and stroke with a healthy dose of Diabetes and high blood pressure (BP) thrown in. I was fighting high BP and arthritis. My doctor said I was doing pretty good, other than my BP and being round.

My Dad was a type I diabetic who passed of a heart attack at 37, his dad died of a massive heart attack at 66. My parents lost a brother I never met to congenital heart issues at three months old, he could be saved now, but not in 1953. My maternal grandmother had three heart attacks and died at 82 from congestive heart failure, her husband, my Papa was lost at 78 from stroke. My paternal grandmother passed at 78 from Alzheimer's. My mother (Muumu) passed at 82 from type 2 diabetes, HBP, congestive heart failure, officially she died after bowel surgery. Three of 4 brothers passed in four years. One at 64 from congestive heart failure, one at 66 from heart attacks and strokes and my baby brother from a heart attack at 48. Sadly, there were drugs and alcohol and a lot of tobacco in their lives. My grands were Finnish Americans so I don't know other family history.

I had a standard BP of 120/80 for years, even when I was in labor. At 49, I wasn't feeling well, my mother told me with my symptoms it was BP or diabetes. I stopped in the local pharmacy enroute to my afternoon shift job as a Control Center Clerk in a state prison, checked my BP, 220/125! I went to my doctor's office; he gave me a script and sent me home. I later learned he should have sent me straight to the hospital. After several months of trying various medications that didn't much help, I went to my husband's Doctor. Some Atenolol and Lisinopril and I was set to go.

The Doctor's Physician's Assistant (PA), had me start on baby aspirin and magnesium. My BP was a constant roller coaster, I was told by the Doctor all the time to lose weight and exercise. I walked and walked, I dieted, with menopause and getting older I got rounder and rounder. When we moved to my hometown town in 2012 my husband, Jim and I began seeing a PA he was treated like a king and I got the standard line about lose weight, exercise and well you're getting older…I walked on… During the pandemic I told the PA that I'd lost another brother, three in 4½ years, she said "Oh, I'm sorry". That was it, never a recommendation for cholesterol meds because that was inching up, nothing. I changed to a different Doctor shortly thereafter, I'd only seen him twice when life struck.

In February of 2023 I noticed that I was getting short of breath and just so tired. I dragged along, I'd been exhausted for some time, I'd sit down and was out. In March I started noticing when I went into work in the early morning, I felt like the cold air was burning my lungs, my feet hurt so bad. A couple of times when I flipped over in bed at night, I felt like my heart stopped and then it pounded. Kinda scary, but everything seems worse at night, right?

The third week of March I actually had to stop walking just to catch my breath a couple of days. I thought I had low iron as I'd had issues a few years back and had infusions.

Nobody is gonna die! …

March 22, my daughter and I were going to leave for a trip from Michigan to Maryland the next morning to visit my other daughter and her grown children, plans made, plans broken.

My husband and I picked our granddaughter up from school (she was 11, we've had her since birth). When I walked up the three steps to the door of our home, I could barely breathe. I tried folding clothes to pack and really couldn't catch my breath, I felt tightness across the top of my chest and in my back. I knew what was happening, but the denial was strong. I checked the ECG on my Apple Watch, it was normal, then there were questions, the result said call emergency services. I told Jim we needed to go to the hospital, he was kinda shocked, of course I said I was showering first. When he told my best friend, since before I can remember. about me insisting on getting a shower she said "that woman is as stubborn as her mother!"

On the way to hospital, yeah, I had him drive me. Jim was fretting and said "I'm supposed to die first! "I told him "Nobody is gonna die today, it's probably nothing important."

At the local ER (20 miles) they got me hooked up and started monitoring me, no one seemed worried. The Doctor told me they were checking my troponin levels and I'd probably be going home round seven. My BP started going way up a couple hours later, my husband ran down the hall for the nurse who came running to my room. They put me on a heparin drip which made my hands turn red and break out. At 7:30 pm the Doctor came in said I'd had a mild heart attack and was going to Traverse City, the Munson Hospital as soon as they got me a ride. Jim went home a nervous wreck as our great granddaughter was at home alone and I called my oldest daughter. The phone tree went into full throttle.

The ambulance finally arrived at three in the morning, I'd been in the ER since three pm and had yet to sleep. They put me in the back and we rolled out, I watched the scenery fly by, past my little town, past my road and had the quickest ride to Traverse City I'd ever had, with the gurney rocking round the curves and the music blasting. The EMS driver had good ole rock and roll blaring on the radio, my favorite, I am a boomer. It was a quick wild ride, we didn't have a siren going, our roads where I am are deserted in the middle of the night and I was stable at that point. It was a 60 mile ride in 42 minutes, fun times.

Saturday…It's the 23rd of March. When we got to Munson Hospital the nurses and ER Doctor did their thing and up to the 4th floor I went. In the morning, I visited by the attending and told I'd get a heart cath after the weekend, and I wasn't going anywhere. I was hooked up to heparin and fluids and bored.

On Sunday the nurse wheeled me to the 6th floor to the cath lab. I was on the table ready for anesthesia and they got word of a critical case was coming in. The Doctor kept apologizing and I told him obviously that guy was in way worse shape than me, I didn't want him to die. This is the cardiologist that I was assigned after my surgery; he apologized a couple times more and told me I'd been so gracious. I was stable, fix him.

Tuesday afternoon I went again to the cath lab, from the result of tests, the Doctor planned on doing one stent. I'd already passed every ECG that had been done. When I opened my eyes in the little room, they had pushed my bed in, Jim said "It's not looking good Gramma, that wasn't long enough." The cardiologist came in with a piece of paper and showed us the results. I had six blockages, two in each of the major arteries, two were 95% blocked, the other one was 80% blocked. Each of the three arteries had another blockage, 90%, 70% and 75%. He told us we were looking at a triple bypass. Jim immediately asked how the hell I was even moving, "do you know how much she walks?" The good doctor told him that's what kept me alive. They wanted to do the surgery the next day but there was no opening and I was stable.

When the cardiac team came to my room later to discuss the surgery, I told them "let's just get it done." The good news was my heart was great, no damage, I had a NSTEMI. So, as I say, I have a good heart, the vein system sucks.

On Wednesday I was sent for vein mapping, it was actually the middle of the night. When the tech told me what she was going to do, I said "oh, just like the leg doctor." Her response was "you've had your legs done? Oh, Doc is not going to be happy!" I told her the veins were all bad, that's why they were done. That afternoon I was sent to second floor where we patients stay after surgery, till we go home. Nurse Angi spent the evening explaining things to me and prepping me.

Thursday March 30, 2023, this was it. My husband arrived at four am as per instructions. Angi got me the orange wipes and I sponged off. I'm generally quite the worrier but I never felt any fear, I just wanted to get the surgery done. As I saw it, there wasn't another option. At about 6 am we were off to the operating room, Angi and I laughed and joked the whole way with Jim shaking his head. At the door I gave Jim my wedding ring (which he wore on his pinky till I went home). Then Angi left me with a wonderful nurse who continued joking and laughing with me. They had me get on the table, put a needle in me and I was gone. As I was sliding away, I said a quick prayer and my Muumu told me "I've got you, you'll be fine."

My husband waited and worried, made calls, answered calls. He thinks it was four or five hours. No one updated him to add to his worries. When they took him to see me after surgery, he said there were tubes and buckets all round me. I was wrapped in a blue bubble blanket and he only touched my toes so he wouldn't leave germs on me. And he went home to worry.

The lost day…

Nurse Angi told me surgery day would be a lost day, indeed it was. I remember so little other than I was groggy trying to open my eyes and that tube in my throat was irritating. Someone pushed me up to sit with a board behind and I thought I'd choke to death. I now know they were doing an X-ray. Later I heard voices around me and I was burning up. I kept writing "hot" in the air with my free hand. Finally, someone said "are you trying to write hot, do you need a fan? "Oh my god, yes please". I got a fan; I still couldn't get my eyes open. When the breathing tube was pulled loose, I couldn't see the nurse, but I immediately asked for ice chips. That was my request every time before Nurse Mason could leave the room, every time. That young nurse is a rockstar, I hope he does well in his career. I was told the next day I had talked most of the evening and was quite hilarious (sick humor is me). I remember none of it. The Lost Day.

I'm awake…

Friday, why does it feel like Thursday? I was so stiff and had tubes coming out of my chest, in my neck and a foley catheter in my bladder. I didn't really feel pain, just weak. One chest tube was pulled out, that felt better.

Early in the morning my cardiac surgeon, Dr. Lall bounced into my room to see how I was doing. I asked her how my prognosis looked. She said "lifestyle, lifestyle, lifestyle! Your veins are terrible, there is nothing left to work with! Diet, exercise, lifestyle, you have to make changes." That kinda humbled and made me feel down.

The aide came in, Katie. She told how I'd been so happy to see her when she'd come in the room the day prior and had said "Katie! It's my Katie!" She had told her Mom I made her feel so good. She was a sweetheart.

I was nauseous and couldn't eat but was starving, more ice chips please! It took a couple weeks to enjoy food but no weight lost.

I was helped to the recliner to try to eat. My daughter popped in and helped me eat my soup, she said I looked pathetic. She called me my mom's name and picked on me about eating tomato soup, she hates it. Luckily, she's an LPN (Licensed Practical Nurse) so she's used to feeding patients. Later the nurse took me walking down the hall, very slowly, not too far. I talked to my daughter quite a while late that night because my mind wouldn't let me sleep. Nurse Angi recommended that my husband get me some low-calorie protein drinks, they really helped because I was starving yet could barely eat.

Saturday. I was moving better, no food tasted good and I was hungry! The last chest tube was taken out. I have a weird sense of things sometimes and the "slurking" noise it made as it rippled over my skin was oddly fascinating. My husband visited daily; my sister came up that day too. My grand couldn't visit because Covid restrictions wouldn't be lifted for a few more weeks. By that evening, I was cruising the hall quite often. That night I was unable to sleep, Nurse Mason got me something for anxiety and said it should help. I had the weirdest, hyper dream and then woke up cold and shaking. The nursing student Abby was in my whacked-out dream, when I told her about it, she laughed and said she'd never starred in a patient's dream before. That night I called the daughter in Maryland because sleep was out of reach.

Sunday. I was tired of being in the hospital. The foley catheter was taken out, yay! The pacemaker wire was taken out, another weird odd feeling. I was feeling pretty greasy by then, no shower since Wednesday night and I have hair that needs a DAILY wash, it was more depressing than anything. I felt gross. I couldn't get comfortable and wanted my home and family. The staff was all busy and everything felt jangled. The day sucked mentally.

Monday. The hospitalist came in on rounds to check on me. He asked the usual questions then asked if I'd had a bowel movement. Nope, then he tells me I would have gone home if I had. That close! The R.N. on duty that day was normally a teaching nurse and was picking up overtime. She had a few tricks up her sleeve and those bowels moved! Just a day of people in and out, to set up rehab, set up appointments. NO shower. That night I couldn't sleep again and roamed the halls. Nurse Mason who had been with me the first three nights was watching and counting laps. I caught sight of myself in the full-length window at the end of hall and nearly cried. I looked so bad! I told Mason I wasn't normally that greasy and gross while holding back tears. He told dayshift should have showered me that day but I would get one in the morning.

Tuesday…going home

The hospitalist came in early and said I'd be going home, Thank you! I called Jim to come get me and bring my stuff. All paperwork was put in order, the wonderful aide helped me shower. The R.N. took the Picc line out of my neck, went over all my aftercare instructions and we headed home.

As soon as we got there, I put my nightgown on and settled in my chair. Jim got the job of getting prescriptions filled, that was daunting. Luckily, I work part time in the store, they know me and they were great helping him. My daughter took two weeks FMLA (Family Medical Leave) to stay with us and it was a huge help. Two days later I struggled into loose sweats and a baggy top. When I came out of the bedroom my daughter said it was a good sign that I wanted out of night clothes.

Eating was tough at first, nothing tasted good and I was so hungry. The protein shakes helped but I wanted food.

Getting adjusted…

The biggest battle was getting my blood pressure right, I had been taken off my old meds and the new ones weren't near as high a dose. A lot of calls to the surgeon's office for several weeks and a lot of med changes. My BP was up, down and round. I developed a terrible cough that ending up sending me to the ER. It was finally decided we'd drop the Lisinopril and use another med. I could breathe again.

The first shower was a marathon, I did it all except dry my back and legs, Jim did that. Each day it got easier, two weeks in a shower was a piece of cake. The hardest part was and still is sleep. The later it got the more my anxiety ramped up. I'm a lifelong insomniac, add in the surgery and I couldn't sleep if someone wasn't awake in the house. I know, fear of dying in my sleep.

My recliner is manual, I slept in it for three and a half months. I still can't lie completely flat on my back; I generally sleep on my side at night anyway. I was trapped at first in my chair begging to have my legs up, then down. Hubby used a length of PVC pipe with a rope on the handle and I was mobile! No pull at all on my chest. He put a hand bar in my shower and got me a grabber to pick things up that I dropped. The staples in my chest and legs were miserable. After 10 days the home nurse took them out, another win.

I got to drive again at four weeks, I carefully got in the pool two months later, into the sauna at eight weeks. I went to rehab at six weeks, all went well. I work part time and took five months off, the day I went back to work I saw my cardiologist after, he was happy with my progress.

The whole thing was harder on my family than me. My grands were worried I'd die. My girls were upset, I never doubted I'd get through it.

The Grim Reaper Lost That Round...
When I say this to people, they kinda think I'm weird, I am, that's life. I much prefer being above the dirt. I'm now eleven months out, I feel pretty good, I'll probably never be a full 100% but I'm about 85-90% and that's pretty darn good. The meds are working, I've lost 23 pounds. I walk and use my Recumbent elliptical daily. I don't have pictures of my hospital stay, never crossed mine or my husband's minds, just as well, I won't forget it. My young coworkers won't let me pick up heavy stuff and every so often I get asked if I'm still okay. Right now, life is pretty good. I'm working on my diet; processed foods are my biggest downfall. I'm not much of a fast-food person. I'm on caffeine restrictions of 16 ounces a day, that's tough for a caffeine addict. I get two cups of coffee a day. I miss my leaded Diet Coke so much. But I have CAD, Coronary Artery Disease, my veins have nothing to spare. My GP told me I have a good fifteen years in me. I told him I needed twenty-six. That got a reaction from him! One of my adult grands when she was young wrote a school paper about the most important person in her life, me, and I would live to be 94. I want her to be right. He also pointed out that I've made it farther than most of my brothers, sadly true.

Physically, I have scars, they're not too bad, except for the divot on the inner side of my thigh just above the knee. The staples looked like a five-year-old was handed the stapler. Otherwise, complaining won't get me anywhere. Mentally I'm looking forward to the next 25 years my grand thinks I'm going to have. The weather makes my chest hurt, I have aches and pain and I now know it's part of a long-term healing journey. Some people say they have depression, mood swings etc… Nope, I'm still as cranky as I ever was.

My message for the ladies, don't let Doctors treat you as less than the men. If you know your family history push the Doctor. Find out what preventative measures there are. Listen to your body! I saw my cardiologist's PA for a regular check the other day. She told me that tests are symptom driven, they not done if you have no symptoms. After watching my BP roller coaster up and down for 18 years it just seems that there were opportunities for intervention. Too late now,

I'm not ashamed of my scars but I wouldn't have them if I hadn't trusted my doctors too much. I felt pretty good so what could go wrong? For starters, those dang family genetics...

Gratitude...

I am forever grateful to the staff at the Webber Heart Center at Munson Hospital Traverse City. I may live in rural NW Michigan but they've got a great crew working there. The good doctors, Dr Lall, Dr Gibbs and Dr Mast are all top notch. R.N.s Mason and Angi were fantastic, (they were assigned to me the most) the aide Katie was a sweetheart. All of the other cardiac team and numerous staff were excellent. I don't want to do it again, but I was in good hands. I can never repay my husband for all of his care and support. My daughter was a great help and the rest of the family was all rooting for me.

Denise Earley, Southampton, England UK

I had my triple heart bypass surgery on August the 22nd 2022. I didn't know what to expect and was scared. I was in surgery for about 5 hours. I remember being woken up by nurses in the ICU and wondering where I was. I think I said to one of the staff am I dead? Ha-ha.

I was in ICU for 2 days before I was taken to my own room. The pain was not nice, there were drips and drains coming out of me everywhere. But gradually they were taken out. They encourage you to get out of bed and sit in a chair and use the toilet if you're able to. It is exhausting and tiring.

The pain from the chest area and my leg where the vein was taken to repair my 3 blocked arteries was sore. I would say except any pain relief going it all helps.

Next the physio staff came and encourage you to walk around the corridor, so off I went with drips and drains for a walk. It is tiring and draining but I managed it. Then back to my room for a well-earned rest and nap. Later you will have to learn to use the stairs correctly with a physio watching you for safety. After you've done that, you will be able to go home.

I was in hospital for 7 days before I went home with my bag of meds, surgical stockings and fitted brace to help protect wound site.

My tips would be except any help and medication that is offered at all times. Another helpful tip is to use a soft cushion or pillow to place across your chest area when you need to cough or sneeze it makes it more comfortable.

Going through this surgery has made me very anxious and afraid. I hardly go out now because i scared of having a heart attack. I only go out if someone is with me. I'm on blood thinners to so try to protect myself from harm because you can bleed a lot and bruise easily.

The whole experience was ok, but it is now recovering that is the worse part for me. I think it's emotionally scared me and I'm currently on citalopram for health anxiety.

Don Helm, Delaware, USA

On February 8, 2023, I had an appointment for my six month check-up with my Primary Care Physician. I had been experiencing some upper chest area pain over the past few weeks but had put off seeing about it knowing my visit to the doctor was coming up.

As a little background at the time, I was 77 years old, male, in what I considered good health, still active and working part to full time. I was an athlete most of my life playing basketball and running 5K to marathons races into my forties. As recently as the week before going to the doctor's I was walking three miles plus on a treadmill at the gym. I was about to learn that no matter what you do you cannot out run heredity.

Back to the pain I was experiencing I had self-diagnosed it, being one of the millions worldwide who had become internet doctors. I concluded I had Pleurisy since the pain was in my chest and seemed to be around my lungs. When I was called back to the exam room, I presented my diagnosis to the nurse who was taking my vitals. She thought it best that she did an EKG just to see what it said. The test was performed and she left the printout on the desk for the doctor. When he entered the room and consulted the results, he shook his head and mumbled, "Umm, umm, umm."

The doctor left the room for a moment and returned to inform me that an ambulance was on the way. He said I needed to go the hospital right away. I replied that was not necessary I would go home do a few things and then drive myself to the hospital. He would not hear of it and shortly the ambulance arrived. I had called my wife, who was at work, and told her what was happening so she could meet me at the hospital.

When I arrived at the hospital the Cardiologist was waiting. He advised that I most likely needed surgery but that a series of tests would be run in the next few days to determine the exact extent of my problems. I was admitted and began the various tests. At the conclusion of the labs it was determined I had several blocked arteries and would need triple bypass surgery. The Surgeon visited me on the 10th of February and after meeting and talking to him I felt very comfortable in his able hands. At this point I think I must have been somewhat in shock because I really didn't have a clue about what I was about to go through.

Surgery was scheduled for Monday morning, February 13th. My children arrived over the weekend to be present for the operation. We talked and chatted and had a pleasurable weekend. I don't think I was having any undue anxiety about the coming event. Monday morning, I got up about 4 am, showered and waited to be taken to the operating room. I was the first surgery scheduled that day and was taken to the OR about 6. The doctor arrived, we spoke briefly, I kissed my wife and off I went.

The next thing I knew it was Wednesday afternoon and my bed was being wheeled to a room in ICU. The surgical assistant who accompanied me asked if I knew my birthday. I responded, after a moment of indecision that it was June 1965. Of course that was wrong I was born June 13, 1945. Next, he asks who was President of the United States to which I answered that I had no idea. This was my first indication that everything was not alright.

Over the next few days, I got enough bits and pieces from doctors and family to piece together what had happened since Monday morning. The operation had taken eleven and a half hours. Every time the surgeon's thought they were finished and began to sew me up the Aortic Valve began leaking. It was somewhat brittle and eventually had to be replaced. In the meantime, I had bled enough that I used every drop of blood available in the hospital. Even though I was the first surgery that morning they had to cancel all those scheduled the rest of the day. I was told that I died twice on the table but have never absolutely verified that information. When people inquire they always ask about out of body experiences. I honestly remember nothing about the operation.

Over the three days I was out of it, I do remember voices which must have been doctors or nurses attending me. I'm glad I slept through those three days. I'm sure it was much harder on my wife and family. Of course, I was still attached to a number of IV's and drainage ports.

The next ahah moment was when my wife asked me for the password to my cell phone and I couldn't remember it. It was a day or two before I could recall it. Over the next couple of days, I slowly progressed to where I was able to go home. At this point I had not seen a newspaper or book or even much TV. Initially my left hand was swollen twice the size of my right and it would shake uncontrollably at times. Please note that I am left-handed so this made eating and doing other small functions difficult.

When I got home my wife introduced me to several Facebook groups that dealt with post bypass recovery and experiences. I found very quickly that I had difficulty reading. This was frustrating because I had always been a reader usually with three or four books going at a time and finishing a hundred and fifty or so a year. Next, I noticed the ticker on the bottom of the TV screen was illegible because all of the words ran together. I had the same problem reading anything on the computer. This was both disturbing and frustrating.

This is about the time I became familiar with the terms Pump Head or Pump Brain. Three common features of Pump Head seem to be anxiety, short term memory loss and long term memory loss. I chose to make an appointment with my Ophthalmologist because I felt like my vision had become worse since surgery. I had previously had cataracts removed from both eyes around 2017. I opted to be able to see clearly at distance therefore I had to wear glasses to read. My reading lens were 1.75 pre-op. When I visited the office after surgery, I was using 2.25 lens and have just increased to 2.50. My problems involving the running together of text etc. has cleared up for the most part. I am able to hit the right keys on the computer key board now something that was extremely frustrating after I returned home.

The biggest problem I encountered with Pump Brain was loss of short term memory. Long term memory returned in a short period of time but short term was a real issue for quite a while. I would read something and instantly forget it, or someone would tell me something and it was gone from my memory in a second. I had to force myself to write down things that I never needed to before. This has gotten a lot better but took many months to start improving.

If I had to offer one piece of advice to anyone about to have bypass surgery it would be to educate yourself as much as possible prior to having it done. There are some excellent YouTube videos and some good literature on the subject. Research things like Pump Head and the Heart Lung Machine so that you are better prepared to deal with things post-op. Also join the bypass groups on Facebook or X.

On a personal note, I was back in the hospital in October 2023 as I once again started experiencing some sharp chest pains. A cauterization performed, after a nuclear stress test indicated some anomalies, it showed my Cardiologist that although one bypass was completed clear two of the others had failed to the point where one was 96% closed and the other was 99% closed. He was not able to get the smallest sized balloon through either one. I met with him and the surgeon on separate occasions and they both said that if the blood cannot get though one way it will seek another path which it has apparently done. It isn't as efficient as it would be with the bypasses open but so far, I am doing okay. I still go the gym every day and do 3 miles plus on the treadmill and a half hour on the bike. I don't do any upper body to avoid the stress on my heart. The doctors seem to feel that I am doing fine and other than a few aches and pains that I think every 78 year old man faces I am truly happy to be alive every day and ready to face whatever comes next.

Kimberley Ann Milley (Morgan), Newfoundland & Labrador, CA
Driving home from work I thought I was having an allergy attack. Turned out I was having a heart attack. I had 6 blockages at the age of 45. 2 stents and one ballon later and I was home. I recovered and was back to work in 8 weeks. I lost some weight, walked 4-5 times daily and watched everything I ate. I felt great.

Fast forward 4 years and I start to feel unwell. It was back to hospital for 3 more stents. The next day I asked my nurse why am I still having chest pain? She said that's just stent pain it will go away in a few weeks.

It didn't and one month later I was back in the hospital again. I couldn't breathe long enough to brush my teeth. At first, they thought something had gone wrong with the stents so they sent me for an angiogram and it was fine. They then said they were sending me home. I had to fight for my life and demand/beg them to do more testing. After many more tests as I was being wheeled into my room only to see 6 doctors waiting to speak with me. I knew I was getting bad news.

I was then diagnosed with Coronary Microvascular Disease. It's the tiniest arteries at the bottom of the heart. When they become damaged, they can cause the same symptoms as having a heart attack. The chest pain is excruciating but lasts less than a minute. I could have these up to 17 times per day. I was then told there is no cure and this is a very rare disease and they didn't know much about it.

I then had my heart medication revamped to add the medication needed to help with this disease and its symptoms to try and control the pain. I was sent home a week later. I was devastated and traumatized beyond words.

When I was first diagnosed, I was an emotional wreck. I would cry any time of day, sometimes little spurts of tears and other times I cried uncontrollably. From my own experience I am a firm believer that heart disease and depression go hand in hand. I have expressed this to my cardiologist on several occasions. It's a form of grief that should not be ignored or passed off by cardiologists.

I was only home two weeks when Covid came. My cardiac rehab was put on hold. For months I wasn't allowed to leave my house. When the time came that people were allowed to get haircuts I still wasn't allowed to leave home. A couple of months later I was allowed to go for a drive but not allowed to stop anywhere. I was also able to walk around my neighbourhood as long as I stayed 6 feet from anyone that I saw. All appointments with doctors were by phone.

When I finally saw my cardiologist in person, he told me that when I was in the hospital, he never thought I was going to live to go home. We talked about how sad and anxious I was every time the symptoms came on. It was like an endless cycle. Symptoms come, my mind would wonder if the pain would stop, if I was going to have a heart attack or drop dead. Therefore, my fear and anxiousness would come. Once the pain and symptoms stopped, I would go back to being myself. This could happen up to 17 times per day. I also experienced night terrors.

He understood and suggested that I seek some therapy to help me cope. I was diagnosed with major depression with anxious distress because of this rare heart condition that had turned my life upside down and inside out. Truth be told, unless you have gone through this no one will ever understand.

I kept asking my cardiologist about work. He kept telling me wait and see. At the two-year mark he told me that I couldn't go back to work anymore. I couldn't be under any stress. He looked at me and said "You do realize that this is chronic and can't be cured!" I just nodded my head and tears rolled down my cheeks. I missed my work life, my colleagues and having a purpose. I truly felt useless. Not to mention how hard it was every day to have to take 17 pills to stay alive. Then along came another big blow.

My partner told me that he was moving out. He said that he couldn't handle coming home every day and watch me suffer. He couldn't handle watching me die. He said he needed some time alone to figure out if he could actually handle my illness. I respected him and told him it's okay if you need some alone time to figure this out. I know that we are all suffering and trying to adjust.

Three weeks after he moved out and I caught him with another woman. He moved out of our house and right in with a new woman. Turns out she was a co-worker and this had been going on for 8 months before he left. What a way to kick someone when they're already down. The next two years of my life were unimaginably difficult. I went to the darkest place in my soul. A place I never knew existed. Not in a million years did I ever think that the person I loved would abandon me when I needed him the most. Not to mention my heart symptoms.

My cardiologist was shocked. He said you're not supposed to be under normal everyday stress let alone this. Doesn't he understand that we as a medical team are doing our utmost to give you the best quality of life that we can!

The first 3 years after being diagnosed consisted of constant med changes, cardiac rehab and learning to accept that this was my new life. Now I'm at the 4-year mark and I've accepted and learned to live with this difficult disease.

Some hard lessons were learned:

- You have to be your own medical advocate. You know your body better than anyone else and you know when something is wrong. Don't let any doctor ignore your symptoms.
- None of us are invincible.
- You can be the healthiest person and it can still happen to you.
- Your entire life can change on the roll of a dime.
- Life is short, tomorrow is never promised.
- When illness strikes, your partner can so easily exit right. It's so easy for them to leave than to be your support person.
- No one truly understands unless they go through it themselves.

How these lessons have impacted my perspective on life:
I let my body be my guide in what I can and cannot do on any given day. If I don't listen to my body and try to push, it makes me listen. It drops a brick wall in front of me to make me stop immediately.
I have no control over this disease or its symptoms, so if the symptoms come on and it means that I suddenly grab my chest in alert mode and stop dead in my tracks no matter where I am then that's what I have to do. I just stand there and concentrate on my breathing and hope the pain will subside.

- I am no longer embarrassed by this.
- I now live one day at a time.
- I made a bucket list and I'm hoping to complete it.
- I tell the people I love that I love them.
- When I hug someone or say goodbye. I hold on a little tighter and a little longer. It could be our last time.
- I am my biggest support system along with my daughter and sisters.

Resilience, acceptance, self-care, gratitude and finding joy:
With the help of my entire medical team, I knew that I had to learn resilience in order to accept my medical condition. One day I looked at my cardiologist when he said do you have any questions for me? I nodded and asked "is this really my new life?" He looked at me with

a sad face and said "yes, it is and now we need to help you accept it." Little by little, day after day I would tell myself this is my new life and I have to learn to accept it. I then went on my self-care mission.

I started by really enjoying my morning coffee, went for a small daily walk, joined Sallie Crawley's heart group on Facebook. Also joined a heart group specific to Coronary Microvascular Disease. These groups have been a lifeline to my recovery. I also have my daughter and my dogs that I know love me unconditionally. I've learned to let negativity and negative people go. I practice being positive and grateful every day. I turned to nature and its beauty to help me find serenity and joy in the little things in life.

As a result of all that's happened to me, I have become more open to accept suggestions such as joining a class on Chronic Pain Management. I practice mindfulness and positivity daily. I've had to let negativity and negative experiences and people go in my life in order to give myself a better quality of life. I have to do what's best for me and my health in order for me to be here for my daughter.

I'm currently working on breaking myself from being the "people pleaser" that I have always been. It doesn't serve any purpose in going forward with my life. I'm going to make the rest of my life, the best of my life! By doing all these things it helps me accept that when God calls me to come home, I will know that I have done my best and that it's my time to go.

Am I scared of this disease? Absolutely!!! I just have to put one foot in front of the other and keep going.

It's funny that when we first get diagnosed, we think it's the end and we'll never get through it. I'm living proof that we can and will endure the hard days in order to have good days and survive. Each day that I wake up I think, I made it to see another day and I'm forever grateful. Am I terrified? Yes, but I can't let it stop me. We only get one life.

Terri Picton-Clark (Dancing Nana), Leicestershire, England UK
My dicky ticker was an inherited condition identified after a mini stroke in 2017 aged 65. I was a very fit retied nana who danced and went to the gym, pumping weight and doing cardio – so you can understand that the stroke was a bit of a surprise and the cause – a half calcified mitral valve – even more so!

My father died of both mitral and aortic valve disease as the condition had been left too long for surgery to have a positive prognosis. Shortly after his death I saw the cardiologist who explained my condition to me and indicated that the aortic valve was involved as well. I was to be monitored until the condition became serious enough to require surgery. In August 2023 I received the news that the aortic valve had left the party and I was to be listed for surgery to replace both valves before Christmas that year, I wasn't allowed to fly and I must admit my breathing was a real problem.

As I was still working out and dancing (albeit very carefully) so I resolved to continue with both activities to keep as fit as possible and keep my weight under control so I would be in good condition pre op. It also gave my mind something to concentrate on rather than doing the Dr Google route and frightening myself. I know that isn't every one's way of handling it but it worked for me!

I was admitted on 27th October for cardio angiogram and listed for surgery on 29th October and was first down to theatre. It is to the eternal credit of both the nursing staff and the surgical team that I really wasn't nervous – I felt included in the planning, had chatted to both my surgeon and the anaesthetist the day before. There was a detailed discussion around the type of valve and I understood that the mechanical valve would probably be unsuitable due to the damage to my valves and that tissue valves would be used.
The op was a long one – over 5hrs – and not without incident apparently. I spent a period in intensive care afterwards, something that was standard for the unit I was in, to allow me to come round gradually and be fully monitored. My husband and son said a

looked pretty white post op and I couldn't string a sentence together. I slept a lot that day but the following morning was encouraged to sort out my tubes and get out of bed into the chair and to walk to the loo as long as I was accompanied.

Post op the best advice I was given by both nursing staff and doctors was to never let the pain meds get low. I found that the codeine derivatives made me feel sick so I was on paracetamol. Anything stronger gave me constipation and, believe me, you don't want to strain with a newly operated chest!

My thought processes were a bit woolly, and I had a very short attention span and suffered from some fairly vivid dreams, 2 - 3 times coming round screaming or gibbering nonsense. Visitors could only stay for a short time as I got tired very easily. I had indigestion and had to change my eating patterns to a main meal at midday otherwise I wouldn't sleep at night. Though earplugs were provided, no one showed me how to best use them so they kept falling out exposing me to the full range of night time noises on the ward.

All was going smoothly when shortly afterward round I began to feel unwell and pressed the call button – it transpired that I was in atrial fibrillation and my blood pressure was all over the place. The next few days were spent adjusting medication to stabilise my heart rhythm – I liked to think of it as a bit of a demarcation dispute between the heart muscle and the new valves as then get to know each other!

There were mood swings and random tearfulness both of which I understand to be normal and a reaction to the body processing the drugs given during surgery, and it does make to feel a bit rubbish at the time. I had to learn how to cough hugging a rolled-up towel to clear my lungs and that coughing happened easiest after exercise.

My scar is really neat running from my clavicle to below my breasts and the breastbone is held together by titanium wires. I did go on a bit about the nature of the scar as my dance costumes often show off my cleavage…….

My husband really couldn't cope with hospital visiting, I think he found it frightening and reminded him of his 2019 admission to hospital after a massive stroke. My son, however, was fantastic! He gave support, reminded me that I had been through major surgery and encouraged me to exercise, mind you he had spent enough time in hospital with various incapacitating injuries to be a bit of an expert on the whole recovery vibe……

My heart rate stable and all other vitals normal I was listed for discharge on 7th December which frightened me a bit as my mind kept doing the 'but what if' scenarios. Again, normal but difficult to cope with. Top tip – no matter how long it takes make sure you know what meds you are taking and when because sometimes the discharge letter isn't clear! It took me a couple of hours to ensure I was doing it right when I got home.

Being at home was difficult, I had heart care attending morning and evening but that ceased as soon as I was able to wash and dress myself. Cooking and shopping became an issue as himself post stroke is unable to organise or cook etc, so meals were a bit hit or miss. We coped – just. My mood swung between coping and frustration with periods of tearfulness and debilitating fatigue. I slept on my own. I had rabid indigestion and didn't sleep well at all. I was angry, frightened and unable to cope – taking it all out on my husband.

But the 'what if' scenario did indeed come back to bite me as I had two more bouts of AF, the first resolved on its own and the second took me back into hospital on my birthday 20th December with a HR of 135 while resting. A period of adjusting medication again and continual ECG monitoring followed with much discussion on cardiac shock treatment to restore rhythm or ablation to remove some areas of cells controlling the rhythm. Luckily for me juggling meds over Christmas worked and I was discharged on medication after the bank holiday with follow up listed.

I am now discharged from the surgical team and back in the care of my cardiologist. I am attending the gym and dancing again. I still can't iron (that's my story and I am sticking to it).

Postscript:
During my clinical journey there were a couple of times when the words used resulted in an inappropriate and totally avoidable reaction from me. Right at the beginning my cardiologist, describing the changes in my heart because of the damaged valve as "your atrium has ballooned". Now as a Nana, I equate balloons with going bang – which of course frightened the living daylights out of me! I did have the presence of mind to ask for clarification, but that phrase still haunts me – especially as my father died of heart valve disease……

The second time was when I was experiencing my first episode of atrial fibrillation post op – I had pressed my call button as I felt very unwell and when the nurse arrived, I was very agitated but due to my high colour didn't look unwell. The senior ward nurse commented that 'you are making a lot of fuss' - my heart rate was racing and not responding to medication and I felt belittled. Let me be clear – at all times I was treated promptly and effectively and just shows the power of words and their consequences.

Communication is fundamental to coping with dealing with the recovery period. My husband found it difficult to understand exactly what I couldn't do. Pre op I was his carer and post op the roles should have reversed but it didn't, resulting on both physical and mental stress. I didn't anticipate or plan for this pre surgery and I should have done.

As you can see, the surgical side went swimmingly but it is the prior planning that will determine the ease of the recovery period!

Jackie Smith, Whittlesey, Cambridgeshire, England UK
My Story: My name is Jackie and I was 58 in June 2022, married for nearly 18 years to Mark and was working full time for a domestic appliance manufacturer in Peterborough. I loved walking and we would do that as much as possible when on holiday. I enjoyed my job, which was desk based but also could be manual and involve a bit of walking around the site too. I was part of a church choir and despite getting panic attacks when singing, I so loved the opportunity to take part. Life was good, normal and apart from medication for high blood pressure and the occasional IBS flare up, I considered myself pretty healthy. I didn't drink alcohol or smoke and wasn't overweight, what could possibly go wrong?

Well, things did go wrong, totally out of the blue one lovely sunny Friday. I had been working from home and my commute at 5pm that day was walking down the stairs where tea was nearly ready. Mark was experimenting with a non-spicy Mexican meal, so nothing iffy there to eat. My surprise after tea was a sudden feeling of indigestion, which was stubborn and wouldn't go with the usual Rennies (indigestion relief). Was it down to the meal we'd just had?

Not being able to settle, I went upstairs and it all went downhill very quickly from there. A sudden bout of diarrhoea came on and then, boom, I felt so ill, all I could do was slide to the bathroom floor. It is best described as a sudden, frightening and brutal assault on my whole body. I felt clammy, light headed, nauseous and had difficulty breathing. I thought about it and discounted a panic attack, so I shouted to Mark that I didn't feel at all well and apparently on telling him I suspected a heart attack (I don't have any memory of that), he dialled 999 and within 6 minutes a fabulous First Responder arrived.

After an ECG, he diagnosed a heart attack and was able to start treating me while we waited another 6 or so minutes for the ambulance to arrive. I was swept up by these wonderful people and taken to Kettering General Hospital, a 45 minute journey, on blue lights and sirens. The fabulous Paramedics helped with my pain, chatted to me and kept me calm and comfortable. After I was unfortunately very sick, they took me straight to the Catheterisation Lab. Again, I was kept calm and as comfortable as possible. A 100%, an 80% and a further little blockage were found and I had two stents inserted. They all had a hand in saving my life that sunny June evening. I said to Mark afterwards via a text, it was like watching a TV documentary, but it was happening to me. Sometimes I still can't quite believe it all happened.

My Musings Post Heart Attack

I have just put together some notes and thoughts. These are mainly things that I found in the early days and weeks after my heart attack. Some of them cropped up when chatting with others at Cardiac Rehab. I found I wasn't alone!

Sleep or lack of. I know I was still in shock at what had just occurred in those last few hours and one thing I was not prepared for was the constant beeping of other patient's monitors. They formed a sort of bizarre repeating tune. And then sometimes I'd inadvertently set mine off too! The other thing with sleep I found was (and I have heard this from other people post MI), that even with being so very tired after the whole episode (in my case it was gone midnight by the time Mark had left), I was terrified of falling asleep in case I didn't wake up again. The lovely nurse looking after me was in and out of the room what seemed like every 10 minutes and once she was happy I was stable, her visits slowed down. I did have a chest x-ray at 2am though! But all through that long June night, which finally turned into the most beautiful dawn, I was petrified. But I had survived the first night!

Loss of appetite. Oh, my word, from the moment breakfast appeared in hospital the first morning, I did not fancy any food. I had to ask them to kindly only do one slice of toast for me instead of two. Only by the third morning, my discharge day, did I suss out that I fancied cornflakes and that carried on when I got home. My poor husband just did not know what to do for meals…anything he prepared I took one look and could only pick at it so not to upset him. It literally took months for me to start to eat properly and there are still some things

I just cannot face, including Mexican food.

Bruising. I could understand the bruising from the PPCI intervention in my wrist, but what was it with all the other bruises that just seemed to appear out of nowhere? My arms and legs ended up looking like I'd been in a fight or attacked.

A dear colleague of mine at work, who had had a heart attack during lockdown, was kind enough to speak with me at length. One of the snippets he told me was that the constant bruising was due to some of the medications I was taking and that it does improve. I can't tell you how much that bit of information meant to me! I was able to pass it on and hopefully reassure others too.

Embarrassment. My knowledge about having a heart attack, well, they usually only happen to men, people overweight, smokers…etc., don't they? I should have known better, after losing my Mum well before her time at 63 from a heart attack which then led to a devastating cardiac arrest. I honestly could not even bring myself to type those two words "heart attack" when letting friends know what had happened. I just couldn't believe it myself. For months I was so scared of it happening again too. Talking Therapy, via the NHS, specific for cardiac events helped me with that anxiety as well as the worry about how to function day to day with whatever the new normal looked like. It was also a Godsend, along with being prescribed an antidepressant, with the surprising and awful deep depression I suffered in the following months.

The witnesses. A bunch of people sometimes get overlooked when a loved one or friend has a heart attack or other sudden heart event and that's the family and friends. I think of my husband Mark who witnessed the event and had to ring 999 etc., keep me calm and then have to travel to the hospital separately as there wasn't any room in the ambulance. He did not even know if I'd made it there for a good hour or so. I think they need help and support too. Mark ended up being signed off work for 2 weeks when all the emotion and stress of what had happened just came tumbling in on him.

Dr Google vs speaking with healthcare professionals. I was discharged from hospital with a bag full of medications and a copy of my discharge notes. Being of a curious mind, I Googled the terminology in my notes, that was an eye-opener. Who knew there was more than one type of heart attack? But it was also a mistake. Other than confirming I had been in a very precarious and life-threatening position; I still could not make much sense of the information and was pretty anxious about what that all meant to my immediate heart health.

This worry went on for weeks until I attended Cardiac Rehabilitation and on the second or third week, with Discharge Letter in hand, I asked if the Rehab Nurse could go through it for me. In those 10 precious minutes, I was very reassured with what she told me and understood much more about what happened, how it happened and how, with their help and continuing to take the medications, things could actually be improved. At Rehab we all were also invited to join the Cardiovascular Disease Education Sessions online, covering heart anatomy, exercise, diet, medications and psychological wellbeing, which were so interesting and again, reassuring, but also realistic.

I would just like to take a moment to say how grateful I am to the Cardiac Rehabilitation Team at Peterborough City Hospital. During the first few weeks after my heart attack, I felt very vulnerable and scared especially when I started Rehab. I should not have worried, because the Cardiac Nurses and Physios were just amazing. Without their support, encouragement and patience, I dread to think where I'd be today. And it wasn't all about the exercise, it was about having the opportunity, if I wanted, to talk with those in the group and to listen to their heart story.

The "But you look so well" scenario. How to handle that when in fact your body and mind are screaming at you and you're barely holding it all together, still trying to understand and process what happened. I know people were trying to be kind, but it was like they didn't quite understand what it is was like to go through some heart related event. Because it wasn't a visible medical thing, like being in a plaster with a broken bone, I must be feeling OK, surely?

The "Well you're all fixed now". Er no. Having to accept and explain the result of the heart attack was being left with heart disease is difficult. Finding myself in a more vulnerable category when it comes to health issues, is sobering. Then there is the rise in travel and health insurance costs, if you can get them. The biggest one is living with the increased likelihood that it could happen again despite trying to follow all the good advice. Quite frankly, it can be a scary place to be.

Life Nearly 2 years on

The "New Normal". This is not about "Look at me, aren't I doing well now", it's more "BECAUSE of all the help, encouragement, reassurance and support I have received, I am doing well in my new normal". I am grateful to be back at work full time, talking full advantage of our ability to work two days at home. This helps me with my physical fatigue and also makes it easier to attend Phase 4 Cardiac Rehab, which I love and is essential for me. If I can't physically do something, I now ask for help. If I'm gone from the office for a length of time, one of my colleagues checks up on me. I'm back singing in my church choir, but now with extra support to get around my panic attacks. Our walks on holiday may not be quite so long in distance, but we really enjoy what we do. We have moved house which, once we got the move over with, has helped so much with our mental wellbeing and stress levels.

I admit, the reality is that some days I feel better than others. The GPs at my surgery are still tweaking my medications and that can be a bit of a challenge. Things can be going so well at Cardiac Rehab. Week after week I feel that I'm making good progress, only for one session where I come away feeling pretty rough with a heart rate through the roof and in tears. I know the right thing to do is to talk to those who can help and support and also not to see it as a set-back. These are only blips that can be managed. Yes, it's tough, but I have to remember not put myself under unnecessary pressure and to be kind to me. There are a lot more positives than negatives!

And finally... **Make the most of the gift of each new day.** So many times this has been said in conversation with fellow heart event survivors and how true it is. It is something I try and do.

Brett White, Missouri, USA

I would like to dedicate my story to my son Greyson; without him I wouldn't have the courage and power to stay strong.

It all started when my mom was pregnant with me, I was born 3 weeks early with an emergency c-section. Everyone always called me a miracle baby when I was young.

I had a normal childhood; I was raised Jewish and followed everything that came along with it. I was never the smartest kid in school, but I always did well. I was very active in High School marching band (Drumline) and even did a summer of Drum and Bugle Corp after my senior year of high school. I always struggled with my weight and have always had high blood pressure.

About 2 months before my 21st birthday I was diagnosed with Testicular Cancer. There was some Cancer in my family history but not testicular cancer. I was rushed to an oncologist, got surgery (Orchiectomy) and within a week I had another surgery and got a port put in and had chemotherapy started. I have 3 full rounds of Chemo took about 3 to 4 months. I spent my 21th birthday with being allowed to have one Beer with my father, per my doctor. Chemo went as expected, lost my hair, got weak, sick and nauseous all the time. Had a few times where I got sick and had to have a blood transfusion.

At my last Chemotherapy treatment, I had an extreme reaction to the medicine. I spiked a fever in the doctor's office, basically started convulsing, and was going into shock. It turned out I had an infection in my port, so I spent about a week in the hospital.

Post that I was told I was clear but would get check up every 6 months to a year. I was so relieved to be in remission.

That next year I met a girl and things started moving very quickly with us.

My next big scare I was around 24 years old my cancer started to come back, luckily this time I just had Laparoscopic surgery had got some lymph nodes in my abdomen removed. After that I was cleared again into remission.

I was still dating the same girl and ended up marrying her and was able to have a son, even though I only had one testicle.

Things were good for a long time we all got Covid once, and it was only a day or two of feeling bad.

At the same time, I lost my job mid-pandemic causing even more stress on my marriage.

We agreed it would be best for our family that me and my son's mom decided to get a divorce.

Around the exact same time we were all out for Mother's Day and I started feeling sick, like I was getting the Flu, so I called out of work Monday and Tuesday thinking I had the Flu. Wednesday morning around 2am I just didn't feel right, my hands and feet started hurting. I woke up my wife and told her I must call 911 on my self-something is not right.

Come to find out my body was going septic, and my aortic valve got infection and it was fused with another valve. I was rushed to a bigger hospital where they were better capable to handle my situation. No doctors could explain how my valve got infected and any doctor or nurse that I saw would check my arms and legs for track marks as I was told this normally only happens from people sharing needles (Luckly that is not something I have ever participated in).

While I was in the hospital, I also happened to miss my son's Pre-k Graduation, I was extremely upset about missing that.

I got my emergency open heart surgery, and everything went well. Unfortunately, since I had an infection in my heart, I had to get a pic line put in arm and had to do 6 weeks of intravenous antibiotics and had to start seeing an infectious medicine doctor.

I also had issues with the tips of certain fingers and my right foot starting to go necrotic. My feet healed fine, and all of my fingers went back to normal except my middle finger on my left hand (after getting the necrotic tissue removed, I have a section of the tip of my finger missing from having lost too much skin).

My ex-wife who thankfully was very understanding and even though she had planned to move as we were getting a divorce, she waited till I was done with the at home antibiotics (that she gave me 3 times a day vs having home health care) and I could drive again.

As my son was starting school and I was soon to return to work from my leave of absence.

We discussed many things about what would be best for us, and our son and we decided together to move from Orlando, FL to St Louis, MO so we all could have a close relationship with our son vs having him have to do long distance.

Well, I spoke with my lawyer told and told him I moved, and I ask him to work out a payment plan for me; which we couldn't work out, so my lawyer dropped me; causing my divorce to be put on hold.

For now, my ex-wife and I live in the same apartment complex (a few buildings apart) (still pending divorce) and we work together to make sure our son can and will have the best life possible.

I may be a fighter and have been though a lot but I can safely say, "My son is the most important thing to me and I will do everything possible alongside his mother to make sure we provide the best most stable life growing up in two separate households."

David Wood, England UK

Upon being told I was very young to need an operation for a valve replacement, I did the BLOKE thing and ignored it and went to the pub.

Papworth Hospital made an appointment for a batch of tests they seemed to take forever but were really only about 40 minutes. About 3 months passed by, then I received my surgical appointment and went into hospital. Sadly, this was cancelled, a further 3 operations were also made and cancelled.

At the second cancelled operation I actually made it to the surgeons table under anaesthetic but as they had an emergency, it was cancelled, I woke up not knowing if the surgery had been done or not.

As I sat in the cardiac lounge the night before my actual surgery, the surgical team came to chat with me and said I'm the 1st in tomorrow. I was then shown to my room and later I got a visit from the cardiac paperwork people, consent forms and risks information etc were discussed and I was encouraged to ask questions.

I had no worries before surgery, everything was explained to me in fine detail including the risks involved. I come from a semi religious background too so I don't have any issues with death.

At 6am the following day off I went, after the surgery I spent a further 24 hours in ICU. I woke up with no pain but very thirsty. I was well looked after and they asked to move my fingers and toes.

I was on my feet day on day 2. After the surgery I had a heart monitor it was no problem. I was paid a visit from the physio team (I think they were used to older people). I had a blood pressure test and then asked to walk up to the end of the ward and back. It was recommended that I should walk around the ward twice a day.

The stitches in my belly really hurt when they were removed, but that took about 10 minutes. I have had absolutely no problems since and the scar is a reminder to me.

Eventually the registrar guy told me I could be go after the pharmacy had put my meds together needless to say that seemed to take forever!

I was told that take it easy for a day or so then work up to a plan of regular walking on a daily basis. I have stuck to the plan. I cycle and walk, although I don't drive now just because, I don't want to.

I now have a little dog to walk she keeps me motivated to exercise, I have osteoarthritis so it's not always easy but I do get 2 or 3 twenty-minute walks per day approximately 1100 steps. I rest in between waking but I definitely feel better for making the effort.

At Papworth Hospital all the teams were absolutely amazing, the nurses and catering staff and the cleaners were 100%.

The Journey: Before and After Your Open-Heart Surgery

"Success is where preparation & opportunity meet." Bobby Unser

An open-heart surgery, heart attack, cardiac arrest or other heart diagnosis can bring a whirlwind of emotions and anxieties, so this book's main focus is as a self-help book for your mental, emotional and practical recovery. I thought it was important to include a little information about what actually happens. Knowledge is power.

This chapter aims to navigate you through the pre-and post-operative phases of heart surgery, demystifying the process and equipping you with the knowledge to approach your surgery with confidence. That said if you have experienced a heart attack or cardiac arrest, likely that you will also have had some intervention but it just wouldn't have been planned so the latter part may be of more interest.

By understanding the process, preparing well, and trusting your healthcare team, you can navigate this journey with confidence and emerge stronger on the other side. This is just a starting point. Each individual's journey is unique.

Remember, open-heart surgery, a heart attack, cardiac arrest or living with a heart condition is a significant but manageable experience.

Preparing for Liftoff: Pre-Surgery

Information is Power: The first step is understanding your specific condition and the type of surgery planned. Ask your doctor detailed questions, gather educational materials, and don't hesitate to seek clarification. Knowledge empowers you to participate actively in your care journey.

Preparing Your Body: Depending on your specific needs, you might undergo dental work to prevent infection, address any pre-existing medical conditions, and start taking medications to optimize your health.

Pre-Flight Checkup: A battery of tests, including blood work, imaging scans, and consultations with specialists, helps assess your overall health and suitability for surgery. Be upfront about any medications you take; this includes any over the counter supplements and address any concerns you may have.

Packing Your Suitcase: Your medical team will provide detailed instructions on preparing for surgery. This includes dietary restrictions, medication adjustments, and stopping smoking well in advance. Pack loose-fitting, comfortable clothes for post-surgery and essential toiletries.

Mental Toughness Training: Surgery and other procedures can be emotionally challenging. Talk to your loved ones, join support groups, or consider therapy to address anxieties and prepare for the emotional journey ahead. While some individuals feel empowered and prepared, others experience fear, anxiety, and even denial. Acknowledge these emotions and seek support.

Pre-Op Jitters: The day before surgery, expect administrative procedures, confirmation of your medical history, and last-minute instructions. This can be nerve-wracking, but remember, the medical team is there to address your concerns. Make sure you tell them how you are feeling, you don't have to be a hero, this is a major event.

Take Off Day: On the day of surgery, follow your doctor's instructions. Trust your healthcare team and allow them to guide you through the pre-operative procedures. You might want to use some of the relaxation techniques that I discuss later in the book.

Recovery Runway: Post-Surgery

Landing Gear Down: You'll wake up in the Intensive Care Unit (ICU) with monitoring equipment and pain management medications. You might feel groggy, have tubes and monitoring equipment, and experience some discomfort. Don't be alarmed, this is normal. Your medical team will be there to monitor your vitals and make sure you are doing okay.

Pain Management: Expect some pain, especially around the incision site. The medical team will provide medications and techniques to manage your pain effectively. Don't hesitate to communicate your pain level so they can adjust the interventions.

Chest Tube Drainage: A chest tube is often inserted to drain excess fluid and air from around your heart. This can be uncomfortable, but it's crucial for healing. You'll learn how to manage the tube and its drainage.

Navigating the Ward: Gradually, you'll transition to a regular ward, where physical therapy begins. This includes breathing exercises, walking, and practising activities like getting in and out of bed. These exercises are crucial for regaining strength and mobility. They might feel challenging at first, but they are essential for a smooth recovery.

Fuelling for Recovery: A balanced diet rich in nutrients is essential for healing. Your doctor will advise on specific dietary needs to support your recovery process as will the cardiac rehabilitation team.
Emotional Checkpoints: The recovery journey can be emotionally challenging. It can bring highs and lows. You might feel vulnerable,

frustrated, angry or even depressed. Talk to your loved ones, nurses, or counsellors about any emotional struggles you face. Remember, emotional well-being is just as important as physical recovery.

Landing Strip: Journeying at Home
Wound Care: You'll be given detailed instructions on caring for your incision at home, including keeping it clean and dry and avoiding strenuous activities that could strain the wound.

Medications: You might need to continue taking certain medications at home, along with new ones to manage pain or prevent complications.

Activity Restrictions: Initially, you'll have activity restrictions to allow your body to heal. Gradually, you can increase your activity level as tolerated, starting with gentle walks and progressing to more strenuous activities with your doctor's approval.

Follow-Up Appointments: Regular follow-up appointments are crucial to monitor your progress and address any concerns. Don't hesitate to ask questions and express any concerns you might have.

Remember:

- Individualised Experience: Every individual's experience is unique. Be patient with yourself and focus on your own progress.

- Be your own advocate: Ask questions, express concerns, and actively participate in your care decisions. Make sure you have the contact numbers for your medical team and especially the cardio rehab team.

- Trust your healthcare team: They are experienced professionals dedicated to your well-being.

- Take things one step at a time: Recovery is a gradual process.

- Setbacks are Normal: Don't be discouraged if you experience setbacks during recovery. Talk to your doctor and adjust your expectations as needed.

- Celebrate Milestones: Acknowledge and celebrate your progress, no matter how small. This will boost your motivation and help you stay positive throughout the journey.

- Seek support: Don't hesitate to reach out to loved ones, support groups, or mental health professionals for emotional support. Do bear in mind that the people who care for you will be worrying and trying to help you by keeping you safe.

It's ALL about You!

"You can only grow if you're willing to feel awkward and uncomfortable when you try something new." Brian Tracy

Welcome to Your Toolbox! You've made it through a challenging experience, and now you're ready to reclaim your life and feel amazing. But where do you start?

Don't worry, this book isn't just about reading, it's about doing. This chapter sets the stage for your personal transformation journey, equipping you with powerful tools and a supportive community.

Throughout the book, there are going to be activities for you to complete. They will be easy and help you to find emotional stability.

You will find space within the pages to keep notes of how your progress is going. It's a real motivator to look back and be able to see how far you've come. You will create a toolkit of your favourite tips to help you be able to live your life happily despite your cardiac event.

So, you don't like writing in books? That's not a problem not everyone does. With this in mind I have produced a printable download of all of the actions with check boxes so you don't have to mark any of the pages.

Download your accompanying workbook to help you on your journey to wellness and happiness.

You can find your downloadable Activity Check List so you can check off as you go without writing in the book. www.myheartandmind.co.uk/bookBTB

There is no rush to finish the book. It's not the reading that will make the difference, it is doing that will create change. There's no magic wand or potion. By deciding to take action and making a commitment, you will design how you want to feel and live your life.

Make sure you come over and join one of my private Facebook groups, they are all closed membership and everyone who requests to join is reviewed before they are accepted so that we can keep you and other members safe.

My Heart & Mind Community for Heart Attack and Heart Surgery Survivors
www.facebook.com/groups/myheartandmindcommunity

Heart to Heart Community for singles living with heart issues
www.facebook.com/groups/lonelyhearties

Smoking Hearts ❣ for the Hearties that want to Quit
www.facebook.com/groups/smokinghearts

These groups are there so you can feel supported and ask any questions you need to. You will be part of a community of people that are all at different stages of their cardiac journey. We will support you

as you work through the ideas contained in this book. These are your hearty communities. Whilst our experiences won't be the same, there will be similarities. In the main, we will all have experienced a life-altering event.
As you read through the chapters and the activities keep mindful of thoughts like 'I know this already'. You could even hear yourself saying "I've heard this before" or "I know this doesn't work" – try to be open minded, interested and take action, don't skip anything. Give it all a go, some activities need to be completed more than once to gain the cumulative effect. Once you've given them a fair go, you can keep doing the activities that make the most difference to you and your life.

Please remember that you may already know what I share with you but have you paid attention and applied it. Knowing is one thing, and doing it is another.

Go Do It!

To feel different, you must commit and take action; this book will only make a difference if you take action. You are worth it; your life is worth it and to feel good now is most definitely worth it. Invest in you, and make the space and time for you to do this. Get a plan and write it down. Be prepared to take action.

Be accountable and make friends with people who have had similar life experiences. Take an active part in my Facebook group and for even more accountability why not share with your family or a friend. Tell them you're on this journey. Get them involved with you so you are accountable to them for your progress.

You could work through this book with a friend or two. You don't have to have had a life-changing event to feel the benefits of the positive psychology in this book. You can just want to create the life you want and dream about.

If you know someone that will benefit either get them a copy book of their own or share yours with them.

And don't feel like you need to rush through the pages. Give yourself a chance to really try out some of the ideas. If you're not feeling it some days don't worry. Work at your own speed and you may find that you want to catch up (binge read) at some point but you don't have to. I will support and encourage you in every way that works for you.

Let's go do this together!

☐ Tick when done ✓

Your 1st Action: Is to join the My Heart & Mind Community

www.facebook.com/groups/myheartandmindcommunity

An Interesting Year - Oh My Life!

"Each situation has a good side and a bad side." Unknown.

On the 17th of February 2016, I was feeling super fit and happy with life. I was at my regular martial arts class (Tang Soo Doo) just about to punch my friend, Nikki, in the stomach, as you do!

As I propelled myself forward there was a sudden snapping sound. To me, it felt like my ankle had been accidentally stamped on. I stopped, and turned around to look but there was no one close behind me. The other sparring partners were too far away to have done anything.

Nikki asked what the sound was but I hadn't a clue. That was until I tried to walk, I had ruptured my Achilles tendon. At the hospital, they plaster cast me and gave me blood thinner to inject daily.

All was as well as it could be considering for the second time in my life, I had a plaster cast. It's all well and good being non-weight bearing, but this time I couldn't even drive as it was my right ankle. Then on the evening of Friday, 18th March, my friend Martin came to visit and we all had a takeaway.

I felt very tired and went to bed quite early. I crawled up the stairs on my hands and knees, I was exhausted. I fell into bed and remembered nothing else until ......

At midnight I was woken with the need to go to the toilet with an upset tummy. I got back into bed with a massive pain at the top of my stomach, it felt like trapped wind. I felt nauseous and rather sweaty, I thought it must be something I had eaten. I spent all night rubbing my tummy and trying to bring up the wind. I blamed the takeaway and swore never to have another one. I took indigestion tablets and ate polo mints, all to no avail; I didn't sleep at all that night.

The next day I felt awful, exhausted and not surprisingly tired. I chose to stay in bed whilst Martin took my daughter to her appointment. On his way back he picked up some tablets specifically for trapped wind from the chemist.

These didn't make any difference; I had lost my appetite and still didn't sleep that night.

I did feel better on Sunday. My indigestion seemed to have abated a little. By now I had neck ache, and backache and my arms felt tingly, I also had a strange feeling across my chest. I put all this down to being on crutches, stress and the lack of sleep.

Over that weekend Martin, my friend had asked if I wanted to go to A&E at least 3 times. To which I said no as I was feeling a little better and thought the aches would go after a good night's sleep.

Again, on Sunday night, I didn't sleep. On Monday morning, 21st March I had an appointment for a plaster cast change. This was for my Achilles tendon. Martin took me and while the nurses were plastering my leg, I told them about my horrible weekend of indigestion and sleeplessness. It never even registered with them that I may have been having a heart attack.

Martin again asked if I wanted to pop in the A&E as we were next door. But nope I was happy to leave. I still believed the strange sensation in my chest and aching arms was due to being on crutches. And I had had a small fall the previous week and had put my arms out to save myself from a faceplant.

Later when I got home from the hospital it was all I could do to lay on the sofa. Martin left to go back to London. I realised that I had 2 appointments the next day. There was no way in the world I wanted to go to them so I rang and cancelled.

After a few hours of laying on the sofa and still not being able to sleep I came to the conclusion that my indigestion and sleeplessness could not be the takeaway. I wondered if I had food poisoning or a stomach ulcer as I had been taking lots of painkillers due to my leg injury.

Eventually, I was so weak I called my doctor and asked for a home visit. I spoke to the receptionist. She said that if I had chest pain and difficulty breathing, I should phone for an ambulance. I explained that I didn't have chest pain as such and I was breathing ok. A little later my GP called to discuss my symptoms before coming out to me. She said she wanted me to come down to the surgery as she could do more tests.

I remember that day like it was yesterday. You know, those moments in life that throw you off balance and make you question everything. Yep, that was one of those days. So, there I was, hobbling around on crutches, and my stomach was staging a rebellion against me. I mean, indigestion, right? No big deal. At least that's what I thought until I found myself in the doctor's office, feeling like I'd just stumbled into a medical drama.

I called up my dad because, well, driving was out of the question. He agreed to be my chauffeur to the doctor's surgery later that afternoon. Little did I know, this routine checkup was about to take a detour into the unexpected.

The doctor examined me and my unruly indigestion. She also listened to my chest and then, out of the blue, she decided to throw my heart into the mix. As if my indigestion wasn't enough drama for one day.

"Let's get you an ECG," she said, directing me to the nurse. Now, I'm not one to turn down a casual chat, so the nurse and I were swapping stories as she sticks the sticky pads to me. Then mid-chat she went silent. Sticky bits were removed, and she left me hanging, literally, as she consulted with my doctor.

Then, boom! My doctor dropped the bombshell – a bleeding ulcer or a potential heart attack. Hold up, rewind. A heart attack? I was ready to sign up for the bleeding ulcer only, thank you very much. I mean, who signs up for a heart attack willingly?

Enter my dad, who was probably wondering why his day had taken this unexpected turn. The doctor turned to him and delivered the news: "Straight to the hospital, no detours." Apparently, my doctor thought Dad's driving skills were superior to an ambulance's speed. Go figure.

At that moment, my life was changing and I found myself facing the unknown. But you know what? Sometimes, it takes a jolt to make you reevaluate things. I could've crumbled under the weight of uncertainty, but instead, I chose to confront it head-on.

Life has a funny way of throwing curveballs our way, and we don't always get to choose the pitch. Yet, here I am, sharing this story not as a tale of woe, but as a reminder that even when life throws you a heart attack, you can find the strength to navigate the storm.

Dad took me to Hinchingbrooke Hospital and I was rushed through as an emergency. I was seen straight away the team were shocked that I hadn't come sooner. I had blood taken and my Troponin level measured, which was over 30,000. They explained I was definitely having a heart attack. They said that I had probably been since Friday at midnight.

After some ministrations, I was sent by ambulance to Royal Papworth Hospital. Blue lights and all, it was like something off the TV, Casualty was one of my favourite TV series. My amazing cardiologist was Mr Will Davis. He and his team worked on me and the culprit which was a 100% occlusion of the right coronary artery in its mid-course. He said that it was a difficult procedure as my arteries were remarkably heavily calcified for somebody so young. I was 51 and I didn't feel very young at the time.

After a few days holiday in Papworth Hospital, I was discharged. I went home initially feeling better than I had been for quite a while and I was looking forward to it. I thought I would come out of the hospital fixed all better, how wrong I was!

At first, I was as weak as a kitten. I couldn't even get all the way up the stairs on my hands and knees. I had to have a rest halfway up. I was breathless and so exhausted. It was hard as I was still on crutches with my plaster cast. As I am sure you know you're not allowed to lift anything in the early days of recovery so it meant I was put in a wheelchair as my body weight was not a good thing to haul around. It's a good job my house was big enough that I could move around. It made making a meal very interesting.

I was in a difficult position of not being able to follow the exercise information in my discharge pack. This was because I was unable to walk. I also couldn't attend cardio rehab sessions and knew no one who had had a heart attack. It was only months later when I was in a position where I could use a bike that I could meet with other heart heroes.

My Orthopaedic surgeon said there was no chance that I was going to be able to walk, run or exercise for at least 12 months so Cardiac Rehabilitation was put on the back burner.

I felt scared, alone and confused. How did this happen to me? I am healthy. I did a sporting activity. I ate a well-balanced diet. I had stopped caffeine over a year ago. I wasn't overweight. I had naturally low blood pressure and I took care of myself or so I thought.

My only lifestyle issue was that I smoked, not masses but around 10 to 12 a day but this was enough. My Cardiologist made it clear that this had to stop and it did! I didn't smoke from the moment I went to the hospital. Not easy but I was determined. There is no way I am going back.

Other issues that may have contributed are hereditary. My mother has had thrombosis and a stroke, a blood clot in the brain. My father had pulmonary embolisms and blood clots in the lungs. It didn't help that I was also on Hormone Replacement Therapy (HRT) as I had gone into menopause quite early in my life.

They immediately stopped my HRT as it increased the risk of more clots forming. It was a bit of a bugger really as it helped me so much, I was secretly hoping I would be allowed back on it after a year. Just as I began to get myself fitter and ready for work, wanting to pick up my life where I had left off in February, I was diagnosed with breast cancer. My cancer was oestrogen-receptor positive so this was likely not helped by taking the HRT in the first instance! So, there was no chance of me ever going back on it, so it's time that I grow older disgracefully.

As you read all that I have been through and with my year being so eventful, you might think that I'm not a very lucky person, I would disagree. It was during my health issues that I came to the conclusion that I was a very lucky person indeed.

Here's a snapshot of how lucky I am.

If I hadn't ruptured my Achilles Tendon, I wouldn't have been on blood thinners. This helped with the blood flow around my heart. I wouldn't have been resting so my heart attack may have been so much worse. It could have happened whilst I was driving or at work.

If I hadn't had a Heart Attack, I wouldn't have had so many visitors. One of my visitors was my dear friend, Dot. She wouldn't have shared with me that she had been recalled back from a routine mammogram. This is what made me check myself.

If I hadn't examined myself, I wouldn't have found the lump in my right breast. Luckily this turned out to be a cyst. The NHS scanned both breasts and there lo and behold the hospital discovered the cancer growing in my left breast.

Even the breast surgeon sees me as lucky. If the cancer hadn't been found when it did it is unlikely that it would have been found for 3 years, my next mammogram! My prognosis would have been very different.

And another upside is that I wouldn't have found my purpose. I wouldn't have known how scary, confusing and overwhelming a cardiac event can be and how I want to give something back and share with you how you can help yourself feel good now.

In the following chapters, you find out about some of the things that I have experienced. Some of the things I have learned. How I helped myself, and some things that others have been through and how I can help you, help yourself too.

Share your experience
☐ Tick when done ✓
Your 2nd Action: is simply to write your story.

What were you doing before, what happened to you, how you felt and anything that you want to include, it is very cathartic. I wrote my story over several days; it was very emotional and yet it helped me get my thoughts in order as some parts I couldn't remember or wasn't sure. I asked others if I needed to help me get a clear picture. Grab some paper and a pen, or get your laptop or tablet, you can even do this on an app on your phone. Just go do it! Remember there is no rush though, take your time.

Life After Your Heart Event

"Take the attitude of a student, never be too big to ask questions, never know too much to learn something new." Maya Angelou

Alright, friend, buckle up because we're diving into life after heart surgery, a heart attack or cardiac arrest. Please bear in mind that something will apply to you and others may not it depends on your experience. I will use the terms interchangeably please use what you have experienced. Because no matter what cardiac event or procedure you have been through recovery is a journey that's a bit like riding a rollercoaster blindfolded. The surgery or procedure has been done, you've been patched up, and now you're on the road to recovery. But guess what? Life feels different. Both physically and mentally. So, what's the deal with life after heart surgery?

Let's start with the real talk – it can be overwhelming, especially if the surgery blindsided you. Recovery takes time, up to 12 weeks, and during this period, your mind is in a marathon while your body feels like it's been through a war zone.

But hey, here's the scoop: life can still be pretty darn great after heart surgery. You just need to cut yourself some slack and give it time. Trust me, I've been there when I had a heart attack, and I've got a few tales and tips to share.

Tiredness Will Be on Another Level

Let's address the exhaustion. Feeling like you've been hit by a freight train post-surgery? Totally normal. Your body is on repair duty, and it's sucking up every ounce of energy to get the job done. And guess what helps the healing process? Sleep! But, and there's always a but, anaesthesia can mess with your sleep patterns.

Listen to your body. When it says rest, you rest. If you can catch some Zs, close those eyes – it's a free pass for your body to recover. Now, if sleep becomes a distant memory even after a few weeks, get moving during the day, with your doctor's thumbs up, of course.

Can't catch those elusive Zs at night? Dark, cool room. No screens. Try reading or soothing sounds. Say no to the blue light – it's a sleeping saboteur. I share more help about aiding sleep in a later chapter.

Soreness, Discomfort, or Pain

Pain after surgery is like an unwelcome guest that overstays its welcome. Discomfort around your chest, back, arms, and shoulders? Yeah, that's the not-so-pleasant aftermath. Follow your doctor's med prescription, move as advised, and embrace that armchair with back support or a well-pillowed bed. Hot water bottle? Your new best friend. Even after the stents I had I felt pain and discomfort at the entry site and yes weirdly I felt like I could feel the three stents in my heart.

Surgery After-Effects

As if your body hasn't been through enough, here come the after-effects. Temperature rollercoaster, brain fog (hello, Pump Head), and constipation – because, well, why not? High-fibre foods are your allies here. And hey, if constipation persists, your doctor might throw a laxative into the mix. Dramatic, but effective.

Depression, Anxiety, and Low Mood

It's not just your body that takes a hit; your mental health might be in for a wild ride too. Depression, anxiety, panic attacks, low mood –

they're all potential passengers on this post-surgery emotional rollercoaster. Recognise the symptoms, and remember, it's okay to seek help.

You might hit moments where you think life can never be the same again. But, let's flip the script – stay positive as much as you can. Positive vibes do wonders for healing and mindset. Talk to your doctor, spill your thoughts to friends, family, neighbours – heck, join a Facebook group where folks have been there, done that.

You've Survived, Now Thrive

The surgery is behind you. You're headed home, to the sanctuary of your own space. Life may be different, and your body sure feels it, but guess what? It will heal. You'll be back to feeling like yourself, maybe even better.

Don't shoulder this burden alone. Talk to your support system – doctors, friends, family, or the friendly folks in my Facebook group. Take it easy on your mind and body. Enjoy being looked after, do things that bring a smile to your face, and for the love of all things heart-related, listen to those doctors!

Remember, my friend, the hardest part is over. You've got this. Life after heart surgery is a new adventure, and trust me, it's an adventure worth taking.

Find a buddy who's walked your path

☐ Tick when done ✓

Action: It could be someone in your life or you could write a post in the My Heart & Mind Community, asking if someone would be there to support you.

Making It Through the Early Days

"Fate whispers to the warrior, 'You cannot withstand the storm.' The warrior whispers back, 'I am the storm." Unknown

Embarking on my emotional cardiac rehabilitation felt like navigating uncharted territory. The day my heart decided to play a wild card and throw a curveball, my world came crashing down like a house of cards. Three stents later, I was released from the hospital, expecting to bounce back with a bit of rest. Little did I know, the journey ahead would be as much about healing emotionally as it was about physical recovery.

Ever been in a situation where you're given the green light to resume life, but the mental fog refuses to lift? You stand at the crossroads of feeling physically capable yet emotionally fragile, unsure about the confidence to carry on after a heart attack or surgery. It's a peculiar kind of loneliness, isn't it?

I remember those days vividly – mentally low, emotionally weak, a swirling mix of confusion, feeling unmotivated, anxiety, and fear. The realisation hit me like a ton of bricks: I wasn't immortal or invincible; I was, in fact, terrified.

So, here's the thing: have you ever been told you're physically ready to head home and resume normalcy, only to find yourself still grappling with a lack of mental and physical well-being? It's like being handed a ticket to life but feeling unprepared for the journey.

Sure, I had the support for my physical recovery. Lifestyle changes and a cocktail of medications were handed to me like a prescription for survival. But, surprise, there was no roadmap for the emotional fallout. That was a journey I had to navigate on my own.

Now, I consider myself fortunate. My background as a therapist gave me a toolbox of knowledge to dissect what was happening within me. I want to share the top tips that helped me weather those roller-coaster days – the days where emotional turbulence threatened to overshadow the physical progress.

So, if you've found yourself standing on the emotional precipice post-heart event, feeling like you've got the physical manual but not the emotional compass, fret not. I've been there, and I'm here to share the insights and practical tips that propelled me from fear to resilience at the beginning soon after my discharge. Because, let's face it, life after a heart episode isn't just about surviving – it's about thriving, and I'm living proof that it's possible.

Facebook Groups

Join a Hearties Survivors Support Group on Facebook. Not bragging at all but I have already told you about mine, we would love to have you join us and you will get a warm welcome.

I'd ruptured my Achilles tendon 4 weeks before my heart attack. So, I had my leg in plaster and wasn't able to attend cardio rehab and I was confined to a wheelchair.

This group literally saved my life. They were a lifeline as my way of connecting with other cardiac event survivors. As I began reading the posts it gave me comfort. I found that I wasn't alone as they'd been through similar experiences and seemed to know how I was feeling.

This group is for anyone who's had a cardiac event and their family. The group was created by Jeff Sykes. I found them on a thread on the British Heart Foundation website.

The purpose of the group is to support each other. To share heart-healthy tips. They also share news and information about heart disease and discuss health issues. Best of all is the great sense of humour and compassion for each and every one of their members.

It is with great heartfelt thanks that I give recognition to Sanjay Shah who helped me in my darkest moments. I posted in a group I had found; I had sat watching and reading, lurking I think it's called. I was desperate I felt like I just wasn't coping and he literally straightaway commented back, we chatted on the group and then he called me using Facebook Messenger. That chat was worth so much to me, it was so comforting to know that I wasn't alone and that I was heard. It gave me the strength to keep going and get to where I am today, right here with you.

☐ Tick when done ✓

Action: I know I am repeating myself but if you haven't already, join my support group the My Heart & Mind Community for Heart Attack and Heart Surgery Survivors

www.facebook.com/groups/myheartandmindcommunity

Cardiac rehabilitation

Whilst in the hospital my lifestyle risks were assessed by the cardiac team. They gave me advice about changes I should make. I was so overwhelmed that I didn't really take it in. I was given a booklet with lots of more information. It included a plan for the first 4 weeks of my recovery at home.

Make sure you read this booklet (and the information about what you can and can't do in the early weeks) and follow the guidance. It is full of great support, information, suggestions and ideas. If you aren't given one then contact your cardiac team and request a copy. Information and knowledge are a useful tool to rebuild your confidence. Try to stay away from Dr Google unless you are on a reputable heart charity website such as the handful that follow, there are more but this is a good start for now.

- Australian Centre for Heart Health www.australianhearthealth.org.au
- British Heart Foundation www.bhf.org.uk
- New Zealand Heart Foundation www.heartfoundation.org.nz
- The American Heart Association www.heart.org
- The Heart and Stroke Foundation of Canada www.heartandstroke.ca

You will be given an appointment for cardiac rehabilitation but it won't be for a while as you need your heart, mind and body to heal. This is really valuable; it's a great opportunity to meet others. You'll learn about how to reduce your risks and exercise your heart in a safe environment so your confidence can grow. Even if you shy away from group things or know what you are doing in a gym, these classes are exceptional and created by specialists who have worked with cardiac rehabilitation for many years.

My cardiac rehab team were a fabulous resource whenever I worried about anything they were only a phone call away, sometimes I had to leave a message but I knew if it were serious to contact the emergency services. They were there to reassure me during panic attacks when I started to feel breathless. I was so hypersensitive to every little thing that happened in my chest that it became my focus all the time.

Your contact list

☐ Tick when done ✓

Action: Make a list of all the contact details of the medical teams that can help you in the early days. Include the cardiac rehab, your cardiologist, your Primary Care Doctor, your pharmacy, etc.

It's good to talk

Talk, talk, talk and then talk some more. This advice was given to me by a colleague from the RSPB who had also had a heart attack, although at the time I had no idea. Thank you, Mark Boyd.

I found this was solid advice. I was amazed at how many people were happy to talk. It's incredulous how many people that I spoke with had also experienced a cardiac event. One day during the first month of my recovery I had a mini mission which was to get my sewing machine serviced. I was getting a quote for repairs to my sewing machine and my heart attack story just came out in conversation. The kind gentleman I was talking to shared his story with me, as he had also had an event many years previously and he made me feel calm and in control and less alone.

Pick up the phone, face to face or online there's always someone. This is another reason to join a Hearties Facebook Support group, there are many of them and all can serve you in different ways. It's empowering to be able to ask for help and advice from people who have been where you are. Don't be scared to admit your fears. Feel the fear and do it anyway - to coin a well-known phrase.

I appreciate that you may not like or find it easy to make conversations. You may feel embarrassed or that your heart condition is all your fault, you may even feel guilty and not want to share with others. I do understand even though I find it easy. I suggest this activity not to make you uncomfortable but to help you process what has happened, trauma is real from heart attack or surgery and speaking about it will help you feel less alone and help to reduce the chances of anxiety or depression after your experience.

☐ Tick when done ✓

Action: Speak to 3 people about how you are feeling about yourself, life and your event.

Be kind to yourself

Remember healing takes time. There is no quick fix; you don't get out of the hospital and then suddenly you're back on your feet. I was surprised at how I felt after the elation of coming home. I was so tired and yet thought I should be getting on with things. I had to relearn healing my mind and body, to put me first and stop racing ahead to the future. I needed lots of sleep, even naps in the day which is very unlike the me before my event. Another reason that we feel tired is often due to medication, it can take a while for your body to get used to the effect so again, take it easy.

It's a huge shock and trauma. One moment all is okay in your world, the next minute you are very unwell and in a serious condition. Take it slowly inch by inch allowing yourself to take the steps necessary to recover. Accept that it will take time and be kind to yourself.

Get plenty of rest and sleep when you need it's your body's way of healing itself. Don't be fooled though, watching TV or reading a book isn't necessarily resting. You are using all your senses as you experience what you see or read. Rest is just being. Being in the now.

Eat healthy foods, take your medications, ask for help when you need it and do as you are advised to by your medical team.

Remember things will improve; the old saying time is a healer is so true.

□□□□□□□□□□□□□□□□□□□□□□□

Tick each time when done ✓

Action: Take regular naps when you feel like it for the next few days.

Emotional awareness

Become emotionally aware! Yes, you were physically fixed when you were sent home from the hospital. Yes, you have medications to keep you well and prevent any future problems. Yes, you have been given information about the lifestyle changes you should make. All these will help to prevent another cardiac event.

But it's the emotional side that can get us when we least expect it. I swung from happy to be alive, to wishing I hadn't survived - it was a shock to have these thoughts. I was anxious, cried for no clear reason and felt angry. These feelings are normal, they will pass. Make sure you talk to friends, family and your doctor. You are not alone, ask for help as soon as you can no man (or woman) is an island.

In the aftermath of a heart attack, the importance of being emotionally aware becomes paramount on the road to recovery. It's not just about monitoring blood pressure and cholesterol levels; it's about understanding the intricate dance between our emotions and physical well-being. I've learned that acknowledging and processing emotions is like tending to the heart's garden – a crucial step in nurturing overall health. Embracing emotional awareness involves recognising the spectrum of feelings that arise post-heart events – be it anxiety, fear, or even a renewed appreciation for life.

One practical and effective tool I discovered is the Physiological Sigh, a simple yet powerful technique to reset the nervous system. By taking a deep breath in through the nose to the tummy, then taking another short sip of air into the chest, holding for a few seconds, and releasing with a long exhale through the mouth making a sighing sound as the air leaves your body. With each exhale drop your shoulders down from your ears. Do this breath 3 times and you'll be pleasantly pleased with how you feel differently afterwards.

NOTE: If you've just had surgery only do this exercise once you have spoken with your specialist team as you will have been given breathing exercises that are of utmost importance.

With this breath technique, you stimulate the body's relaxation response. It's a gentle reminder that, amidst the chaos of emotions, there's a calm within reach. Incorporating emotional intelligence and tools like the physiological sigh into the recovery process has been a game-changer, fostering not just physical healing, but a holistic and resilient approach to life after heart surgery or a heart attack.

☐ Fill in the table below each time you use it ✓

Action: Use the Physiological Sigh each time your feelings start running away with you. Each time write how you felt before you did it and how you felt after you had completed it.

How did you feel before?	How do you feel afterwards?

Be in the now

Try to be in the present moment, in the now. The past has passed and the future has yet to happen. The present is a gift.

You can't change what happened in the past, and worrying about the future won't change it. Stay focused on the now, and take each day as it comes. Live in each moment as it happens.

Learn meditation or find out about mindfulness. These are practices that will help you immensely. I used meditation daily for 10 minutes. The good stuff doesn't happen while you meditate. It's cumulative and will make a difference in keeping you calm and relaxed with a positive mindset.

Another simple technique is the spiral of twelve. You can do this any time, any place and anywhere.

The spiral of twelve

Using the pad of your thumb of the same hand touch the pad of each finger in the order of the numbers. See the image below for the order. Do this once, twice, thrice and then repeat as required. This will help ground you and calmly move your focus.

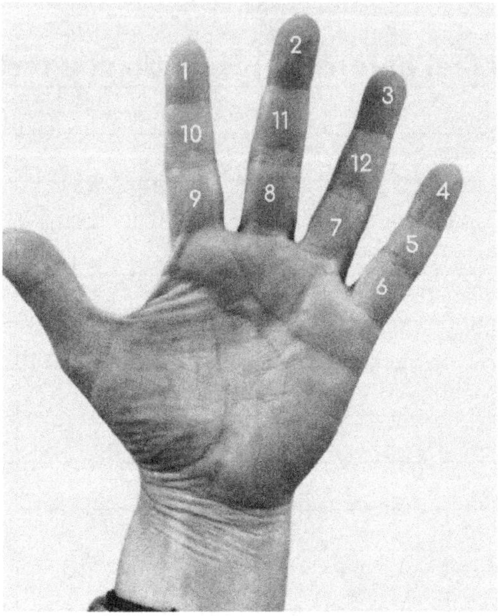

There's more information about managing anxiety on my website and there is also a free download to help you.

☐☐☐☐☐☐☐☐☐☐☐☐☐☐☐☐☐☐☐☐☐☐☐☐☐☐☐☐
Tick each time you've used it ✓
Action: Use the spiral of 12 when you start to worry.

Use your recovery time

Make the most of your recovery to do something that you haven't done before. How about binge-watching a television series that you've always wanted to watch on Netflix?

Start reading a book? How about doing a jigsaw puzzle or starting something creative that you've never done before? Painting or drawing? Maybe there was something you loved doing but as life got

so busy you stopped doing it. Crafting, Lego, model making, knitting or crochet perhaps. What about photography whilst you are building up your walking?
Think about what you quite fancy doing. It doesn't have to be anything that you are good at just something that gives you pleasure and enjoyment.

My guilty pleasure was that I watched every single episode of Chicago Fire back-to-back - not sure it did my heart any good with all the cliffhangers and drama. But it sure took my mind off the here, the now, the future and the past (and Kelly Severide is total eye candy).

☐ Tick when done ✓
Action: Make a list of things you can do that bring you pleasure and happiness.

Friends and family
Spend time with people you love. Reach out to those who make you happy, who support you and who love you.

Remember that some people just don't know what to say, and so are scared of getting in touch with you. Make it easy for them, you need them to understand you but you also need to understand them.

If you have pets, make some time to spend stroking and caring for them, the therapeutic effect is well known. Being loved and giving love is one of the best ways to heal yourself.

Don't confuse people who are always around you, with people who are always there for you. You will be pleasantly surprised at the people who become closer.

Surround yourself with people who make you hungry for life, make you laugh, who touch your heart and nourish your soul. Positive people zone only.

☐ Tick when done ✓

Action: Make a list of all the beings that make you feel good, send them a text, make a call or arrange for them to visit – with or without pets your choice.

Set mini-missions for the day

Once you are feeling stronger and feeling like you can do a little more each day. Start to set yourself goals, simple little goals. Use a journal, your phone or a scrap of paper to capture them so you know what you have in mind.

Start with small achievable and measurable goals. In the early days, for me, it could be as simple as just going downstairs and making yourself a cup of tea (remember I couldn't walk due to rupturing my Achilles). Gradually day by day you'll be able to achieve more and make your goals slightly bigger and more of them. The information you received on leaving the hospital from the cardiac team is a good starting place for what you can start doing and when.

My mini missions started as getting downstairs, having breakfast, meditating, having lunch, watching Chicago Fire and getting to bed. I then started to build in other things and my first big (for me) achievement was spending 15 minutes a day to read and then action my emails. I found at first it was incredibly tiring but I felt a sense of accomplishment once I had finished. In time it built up until it was just a normal part of my day.

☐ Tick when done ✓

Action: List your missions and keep them on hand. Do not allow this to be a long to-do list though, that can come later.

Find the treasure

Look for the positive in your recent experience. It was a shock, terrifying and no doubt life will never be the same. But that doesn't mean it can't be different or even better! I know my life is greatly improved.

Spend time thinking about what you have been through and notice any differences. There will be something good that has come out of this. You may not see it right now but keep looking and I am confident there will be something.

I no longer suffer fools. I make the most of each and every day. I see my cardiac event as a warning to remind me to make a difference and change my life. I learnt that it's experiences and people that make my life fulfilled.

☐ Tick when done ✓
Action: Review your heart story from the early chapter. Actively look for all the positives that have come from your event and during your recovery.

Find a purpose
Studies show that those with a purpose live longer, sleep better and have a more robust immune system, lower stress levels and better cognitive function. Take your recovery time as an opportunity to look for purpose or meaning outside of yourself and your situation. Think about some things that you can do to help or serve others. It could start as a mini mission that you can build on or something for the future when you are able to take on more, try coming up with as many ideas as possible.

Is there a charity that you could get involved with, maybe starting where you can volunteer from home? Is there something that you can do that helps in your local community? Is there something that you could contribute? Such as writing an article for your local newsletter. Even by joining an online group and replying to someone who needs help and support, you can help them and feel good yourself.

☐ Tick when done ✓
Action: Make a list of things that you can do now, that will give your day's purpose.

Empower Your Life

"Writing is medicine. It is an appropriate antidote to injury. It is an appropriate companion for any difficult change." Julia Cameron

Empowering yourself is not just a good thing; it's the key to reclaiming control and finding strength amid the challenges of living with heart disease. When you face such a formidable adversary, like a heart condition, it's easy to succumb to feelings of helplessness.

However, self-empowerment becomes a beacon of light in the face of adversity. It's about acknowledging that, despite the diagnosis, you still have immense power over aspects of your life. And here's where the humble journal becomes a potent ally. It's more than just a collection of words on paper; it's a tangible tool for self-reflection, growth, and resilience. Journaling allows you to chronicle your journey, track your emotional landscape and identify patterns that might be affecting your well-being. It becomes a companion in navigating the emotional highs and lows, providing a safe space to express fears, hopes and triumphs. In the process, you transform from a passive observer of your situation to an active participant in your healing journey, gaining a sense of empowerment that can be truly transformative.

I found that in the early days, I didn't want to just freestyle my journaling. I knew keeping a journal or a diary helps you keep focused and move forward. So, I decided that it didn't have to be very long, just enough to keep me aware of how I was improving day by day. I created my own journal with specific prompts. I share this with you as I found it very useful.

By using the journal prompts daily will help you become your best self. You'll adopt a positive outlook on life, practice gratitude and reflect on your growth one day at a time. You can write about what you have achieved, how you are feeling and rate them on a scale of 1 -10. You can use it to capture your thoughts about all the things that you might want to discuss. It will help you be able to share them with the important people in your life. You could even start a bucket list of all the things you want to do in the future.

Having gratitude is an important part of mental well-being and healing. I found it incredibly useful to sit each evening and write a list of 5 positive things that had happened that day or that I was grateful for. Sometimes it would be something small like the sun shining or that I was grateful for my mobile phone. At other times it was about huge things like being able to walk for half an hour. Try not to repeat yourself though, look for all the little things that make you happy. A free refill of coffee or someone smiled at you.

Journaling

At the end of this chapter, I have included 7 samples for you to use starting today. Here is a link to download some more printable A4 journal pages so you can continue as I am going to ask that you do this for 4 weeks.

www.myheartandmind.co.uk/bookBTB

You don't have to use my template so you can create your own. So, when you're ready you can start now, turn over and begin completing your journal or use your own ideas. I suggest not looking at each day's journal until the end of each week. It will help give your perspective about how things are going for you

Here are the prompts that I use and what I include in each section.

Now: Write the day and date. Also add one word that describes how you feel in this moment.

Purpose: What 1 thing are you going to achieve today? That no matter what, you are going to do it.

Belief: What is your mantra for today? Choose an affirmation and commit to saying it 3 times over throughout the day. It can help to anchor it to another activity such as whenever you walk through a doorway or when you make a cuppa.

Thoughts: Freely express how you feel and what you think with no censorship. Journaling is often thought of as a thing that is more for females and is a bit spiritually out there! Let me tell you it is not, there is science behind it and it's not just for the ladies. My friend Jon Johnson, a fellow heart attack survivor and author told me when I interviewed him for my podcast, that he calls it 'pooping on paper' and it helped his recovery tremendously.

Then review your words and you have 2 options: a) You can leave it as it is, if your words are in the main positive and uplifting or b) If they aren't helpful, kind or useful, consider how you can change them to make you feel better.

Future: What do you want to do in the future? What are your goals, your dreams and ambitions? Add anything that you would like to experience, be, have, do, see or hear. There's nothing too big or anything too small.

Gratitude: At the end of the day list 5 positive things that have happened today or that you are grateful for. Remember that sometimes it is the little things that bring the most pleasure.

Achievement: Write 3 things that you have completed today. Big or small they all count; it could be 15 minutes of managing your emails or doing the washing up.

☐ Tick when done ✓

Action: Keep a daily journal for this week and encourage yourself to keep that streak going.

To continue for the next three weeks or if you enjoy this process and wish to continue you can download a FREE printable template file here
www.myheartandmind.co.uk/bookBTB

Daily Empowerment Journal

NOW today is:

PURPOSE today I will achieve?

BELIEF today's affirmation is?

GRATITUDE today's great because?

JOURNALING about today?

ACHIEVEMENT today I did?

FUTURE to do, see, be, have or hear?

Daily Empowerment Journal

NOW today is:

PURPOSE today I will achieve?

BELIEF today's affirmation is?

GRATITUDE today's great because?

JOURNALING about today?

ACHIEVEMENT today I did?

FUTURE to do, see, be, have or hear?

Daily Empowerment Journal

NOW today is:	
PURPOSE today I will achieve?	BELIEF today's affirmation is?
GRATITUDE today's great because?	JOURNALING about today?
ACHIEVEMENT today I did?	FUTURE to do, see, be, have or hear?

Daily Empowerment Journal

NOW today is:

PURPOSE today I will achieve?	BELIEF today's affirmation is?
GRATITUDE today's great because?	JOURNALING about today?
ACHIEVEMENT today I did?	FUTURE to do, see, be, have or hear?

Daily Empowerment Journal

NOW today is:

PURPOSE today I will achieve?

BELIEF today's affirmation is?

GRATITUDE today's great because?

JOURNALING about today?

ACHIEVEMENT today I did?

FUTURE to do, see, be, have or hear?

Daily Empowerment Journal

NOW today is:

PURPOSE today I will achieve?

BELIEF today's affirmation is?

GRATITUDE today's great because?

JOURNALING about today?

ACHIEVEMENT today I did?

FUTURE to do, see, be, have or hear?

Is Anxiety Good or Bad?

"You don't have to control your thoughts. You just have to stop letting them control you." Dan Millman

A touch of anxiety can act as a built-in alarm system, keeping us alert and responsive. We experience it as our mind's way of keeping us safe and ensuring our survival. However, when anxiety takes the reins and gallops into the realm of excess, it transforms from a helpful nudge to a relentless storm, wreaking havoc on both physical and emotional well-being.

This is particularly significant for those living with heart disease, as excessive anxiety can mirror the symptoms of a cardiac event, with panic attacks often masquerading as the real deal. In the aftermath of a cardiac episode, hypervigilance becomes our unwelcome companion, heightening sensitivity to every bodily sensation. I, too, found myself in a constant state of worry, questioning the arrival of another heart attack.

The cascade of stress hormones, adrenaline, and cortisol triggered by anxiety sets off a physiological response known as the fight or flight reaction, resulting in an increased heart rate, palpitations, and heightened sweating. Prolonged exposure to these hormones can leave one feeling perpetually on edge, struggling to concentrate, irritable, tearful and plagued by sleep difficulties. Yet, there's a silver lining – the recognition of these symptoms opens the door to simple yet powerful techniques that can effectively quell anxiety and stress, providing a lifeline for those navigating the intricate landscape of life with heart disease.

Here are some quick tips to help you to tame those butterflies in your tummy.

Breathe

Repeat this breathing exercise 6 times as a set. Follow your breath as it flows in and out. Do not try to control your breath. This is a good way to relax during any activity and when other people are around as it's not obvious what you are doing.

- Breathe in through your nose slowly and deeply to the count of 6.
- Imagine breathing in peace and calm.
- Hold for the count of 3 as you take a moment.
- Then exhale through your mouth to the count of at least 6.
- Feel all of the tension and anxiety flowing out of you as you let the breath go.

Then allow yourself to find a breathing pattern that is natural and relaxing for you. Please always check with your medical practitioners if you have recently had heart surgery or a heart attack. Always follow medical advice,

☐ Tick when done ✓

Action: Try this technique next time you feel anxious, stressed or overwhelmed.

Mind-body connection

Science has proven that how we arrange our bodies affects how we feel about ourselves. After heart surgery or a heart attack, our bodies are usually feeling like they've been worked over by Mike Tyson. It takes time for us to heal and sometimes it means we adopt a posture that isn't beneficial for us.

Living with heart disease can be very stressful and cause anxiety, we tend to take on the body position of a victim because of pain either emotional or physical. This in turn can affect our thoughts. When we sit up straight, we are more likely to remember positive memories and think of something positive. The way we stand, sit, and walk, actually affects our mood and happiness.

Try this technique, but only under the advice of your medical team, you need to know you are physically fit before undertaking certain movements.

- Take gentle breaths in and breathe out slowly as you do this
- Begin by dropping your shoulders down and allowing them to move a little backwards
- This will start to raise your chest so be careful
- Notice your head and lift your chin up
- Pay attention to your mouth let your tongue relax
- Then release your jaw, letting it drop gently
- Have a little wiggle and allow yourself to stand or sit tall
- And a final deep breath in, hold a moment, exhale slowly and begin sighing as the air leaves your body

Give this a go whenever you are feeling down in the dumps, feel like a victim or have a brain fog moment it helps clear your mind and grow your confidence.

☐☐☐☐☐☐☐☐☐ Tick when done ✓
Action: Practice connecting your mind and body 9 times over the coming days.

Reduce stimulants
Make the decision to avoid caffeine, alcohol, fizzy sweet drinks and large amounts of sugary sweets.

You may believe the extra rush from a cup of coffee, a glass of alcohol or a helping of cake will make you feel better and give you more energy. It will at first but it's short-lived after the initial hit it's all downhill.

Stimulants can also aggravate the symptoms of anxiety due to the effects they have on the nervous system. The same applies to nicotine. Coffee and booze will affect your sleep so limit or stop until you're feeling better. They can also cause palpitations which can start the worrying and anxiety cycle.

☐ Tick when done ✓

Action: Review how much caffeine, sugar, alcohol or nicotine you have and look at where you can reduce consumption.

Befriend your heartbeat

This might sound crazy, but hear me out. If hypervigilance of what is going on in your chest is making you anxious and you're freaking out about every thump and flutter I suggest starting to make friends with your heartbeat. Imagine it as a drumbeat, a steady rhythm guiding you through your day.

Think about your circumstances, have you just exercised or exserted yourself or had a cup of coffee? Is it a little fast? Maybe take a few deep breaths and relax down. But focus on that steady pulse, a reminder that your amazing heart is working hard to keep you going.

You may want to check your BP, HR and O^2 for reassurance, I did in the early days.

However, if in any doubt, then do check it out and contact your emergency services.

☐ Tick when done ✓

Action: Notice what your chest and heart feels like when you're feeling okay, remind yourself when you're feeling anxious that prior to your event/surgery you weren't paying as much internal attention and relax to the sound of your drum.

Who are you talking to and what are you saying?
Do you talk to yourself? I do, I found that my thoughts really influence how I feel. Stop for a moment what is your inner voice saying? What are you saying or thinking to yourself? If you wouldn't say it to a friend, don't say it to yourself.

During my recovery, I spent a long time ruminating about the past what I should and should not have done that could have prevented my heart attack. I thought about all the things that I could no longer do due to my health predicament. I felt guilty, I felt angry, I felt let down by my body, I didn't trust myself, I worried about the future and all the things that I couldn't control. It just made me miserable.

Over the next couple of days pay attention to how you are feeling. Chances are if you are feeling happy and content you will have been thinking good thoughts about yourself and your life. If you are feeling anxious or angry then your thoughts are most likely going to be negative and make you feel like a victim.

If your self-talk is less than useful, has any negative impact and makes you feel unhappy. Tell yourself to "shut the hell up'. Then move your focus on to more positive thoughts, and find something that is more useful and helpful to say to yourself. Change your inner dialogue to useful phrases such as 'I can handle this' and 'What can I do next'.
It's not always easy to maintain a positive mindset and nor should we be looking to achieve this all the time. However, this is something you can use at the moment when you are feeling overwhelmed and anxious.

☐ Tick when done ✓
Action: Use your journal to start to identify what you are saying in your thoughts and how you are feeling at that moment.

Lavender
The origin of the use and benefits of Lavender goes back some 2,500 years in history; it is one of the most versatile essential oils. It may be useful for treating anxiety, insomnia, depression, and restlessness.

It is physically and emotionally calming, relaxing and balancing.

You can burn incense or candles. Sprinkle a few drops of oil on a cushion/pillow or use a hot stone or oil burner. For an immediate calming effect rub a few drops of the oil into your cupped hands. Inhale deeply drawing the scent into your amygdala (the emotional warehouse) to calm your mind and body. I grow it in my garden and when I brush past it is heavenly. I dry it and then sprinkle it crushing the flowers when I need a lift in my home.

☐ Tick when done ✓
Action: Get yourself some lavender smellies.

Gratitude graffiti
Okay, this one doesn't involve actual spray paint (unless you're feeling particularly artistic!). But the idea is to write down things you're grateful for – big things, small things, anything that brings a smile to your face.

Stick them on your bathroom mirror, the fridge, the wall in front of you, your boxes of tablets etc., anywhere you'll see them throughout the day. Those little reminders of the good stuff in life can seriously shift your perspective and melt away worry.

☐ Tick when done ✓
Action: Find some post it notes and coloured pens so you can start writing down your gratitude.

Move your body
We all know that exercise increases your physical health and emotional well-being, it puts more pep in your step every day. It has some direct stress-busting benefits as it pumps up your endorphins. However, after a heart attack or heart surgery exercise is not an option in the short term.

However, it is a good thing to move your body around even if it is just in parts. It helps to move your personal energy around the body and works as a distraction too.

If you find you are caught up in anxious thoughts stand up and move around. Shake yourself out of it. Do a full-body shake or tremble. If you can and have checked with your cardiac team hop, skip or jump for a few moments if you can. If you are seated then try waving your arms around and opening and closing your fists. Shake your legs, scrunch up your toes and wiggle your head from side to side on your neck. Let your own feel-good chemicals release and move around your system.

Okay, so going to the gym, for a run or your preferred aerobic exercise is off the cards for a while. But you could (after checking with the medical team) take a brisk walk up and down the stairs a couple of times. Better still chuck on some tunes and dance it out for a few minutes.

Just going out for a walk, which we all must do to aid our cardiac recovery is enough to get the energy moving around you.

□□□□□□□□□ Tick when done ✓
Action: Shake it out of your body when you feel anxious, give it a go on 9 occasions. But only once you have checked with your medical practitioner.

Time to unwind
This is another mind-body activity that utilises your imagination. It is best to read through it a few times so you feel more familiar with it. It can also help with food, nicotine or alcohol cravings.

- Once you realise you are feeling anxious or uptight. Notice the anxiety/uptightness as a sensation within your body (maybe in your tummy, chest, head or mouth).
- Imagine pushing it out of your body as a shape. It can be any shape that feels appropriate it's not real you are using your creative imagination.

- In your imagination change the shape to a smoother, calming and more comfortable shape.
- Start to notice in your imagination what colour the original shape was and now the new shape is. You can now change the colour to something that makes you feel soothed and calm.
- Now you've got that new shape in your mind's eye, I want you to imagine seeing the shape spinning in front of you, pay attention to the direction of the spin. Left, right, forward or back, maybe on the diagonal?
- Using your powerful and unlimited imagination I want you to visualise changing the direction of the spin so it's spinning the opposite way to how it was originally. Yes, that's right.
- You can next, see in your mind's eye pulling the spinning shape you have just created back inside you. As you do now
- Notice how the feeling is moving down and changing as you feel even more relaxed and more at ease.
- You can, can't you already, begin to spin the shape faster and faster. Even faster. So fast now that it reduces to nothing a tiny dot of nothingness. Or expands exploding into dust as it disappears completely. Which one happened for you?
- How much better are you already feeling right now!

□□□□□□□□□ Tick when done ✓
Action: Read through the activity instructions and use them on 9 occasions. It truly is amazing and will make a huge difference to your thoughts and feelings.

Nurture your green spirit
We all know plants are good for the air, but did you know they're good for your stress levels too?

I started surrounding myself with greenery. A little fern on my desk, a climbing ivy in the corner – it's amazing how the act of caring for another living thing (even if it's pretty low maintenance) can be calming. Plus, studies actually show that being around nature reduces stress hormones!

☐ Tick when done ✓

Action: Find yourself a small houseplant to look after, you can also talk to the plant too as it is said it helps them grow.

Take a mental holiday

Take a mental holiday once a day. This is a little like a cross between meditation and self-hypnosis. If you can't get away physically whether that is just changing the room you are in or going outside, then an imaginary holiday will do you the power of good. Relaxing breaks such as these have been found to help recovery by returning our mental and physical systems to their baseline.

Get yourself comfortable and relax your jaw and your shoulders. Place your feet flat on the floor; and your hands loosely on your lap. Close your eyes, and concentrate on your breathing for a few breaths.

In your imagination take yourself off to your favourite place. Somewhere you enjoy being and you feel safe and calm. Maybe a beach, woodlands, snow slopes, a park, a field in the country, in town or in the city as long as it's somewhere that is your happy place.

Imagine all the little details, what you would see, hear, smell and feel. Sometimes it can help to listen to some background sounds that remind you of that place, there are plenty on YouTube.

As you become more relaxed start saying 'I feel good' over and over gently in your mind. If your mind wanders off, gently notice accepting that it is okay and then take your thoughts back to your favourite place and the words 'I feel good'.

Whilst this technique will help in the short-term changing how you feel it is the long-term effects that are most useful. By practising a technique like this regularly you start to re-programme your ability to relax and feel safe and secure. It's the cumulative effects of doing this regularly that will cause better results, again this is much like meditation.

☐☐☐☐☐☐☐☐☐☐☐☐ Tick when done ✓
Action: Take a mental holiday every day for 12 days in succession.

Embrace the power of "no"
This might be the hardest one, but it's incredibly important. We all have a limit, and saying no to things that drain our energy or make us anxious is crucial for self-care. It doesn't make you a bad person, it makes you a smart one who prioritizes your well-being. Learning to set boundaries might feel strange at first, but trust me, the peace of mind it brings is worth the initial awkwardness.

☐ Tick when done ✓
Action: Pay attention to the people and things that you wish you'd said no to that are causing you to feel anxious. Is it time for you to start setting boundaries? Remember, no is often for right now and you are free to change your mind at another time.

Changing How You Feel About Pain

"The great art of life is sensation, to feel that we exist, even in pain."
Lord Byron

Experiencing aches and pains post-major heart surgery is practically a rite of passage. Your back, neck, shoulders, and even the front of your chest can become a symphony of discomfort, all thanks to the muscles and ligaments doing their stretching routine during the operation.

Let's talk about those moments of brief, sharp pains flanking your chest – like unwelcome party crashers. The good news? Usually, these sensations only last for around 4 to 6 weeks. But, and it's a big but, not every post-surgery chest sensation is a nod from the universe saying, 'Hey, everything's fine.' If you feel anything resembling chest pain or pressure during exertion, consider it your body's red flag – consult your medical team or call the emergency services as soon as possible.

Now, when it comes to having stents after a heart attack, the grapevine might tell you there's little to no pain involved. Reality check: you might face some soreness and discomfort, especially around the entry site. And don't be surprised if your stent takes a bit of time to settle in – it's like a houseguest making themselves at home. Personally, I had this odd discomfort lingering for about a week whenever I lay on my left side in bed. Supposedly normal, but hey, if it's playing on your mind, dial up your medical team.

So, let's dive into the fascinating world of pain. It's not just a sensation; it's a message from your body, a signal that something's wrong. Your body shouts, 'Danger!' and your mind takes the reins on what to do about it. But here's the kicker – sometimes this communication system goes haywire. In emergencies, you might feel no pain at all, while amputees can experience phantom limb pain – a twisted game of telephone between body and mind.

Now, I'm no stranger to this dance between body and mind.

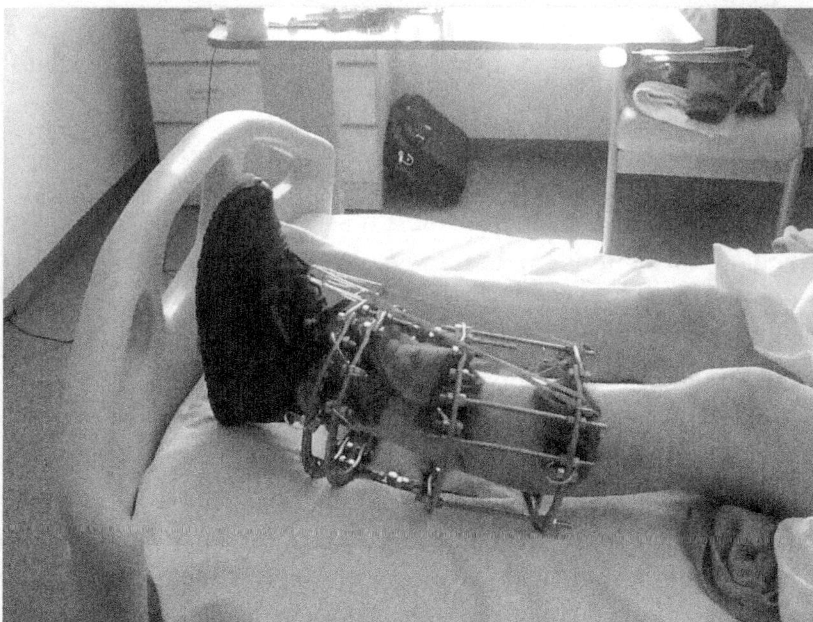

I had my own journey through post-surgery discomfort when I had my leg reconstructed, it opened my eyes to the power of the mind in controlling pain. And here's the best bit: not every solution to pain needs to be a prescription. There are natural methods, little hacks if you will, that can help you weather the storm of discomfort and manage pain without solely relying on medical interventions.

It is a case of different strokes for different folks though. Read on and try some of these techniques out, you've nothing to lose and everything to gain.

Four square breathing

Numerous studies have been done to determine if 4 square breath work can help relieve pain. Some studies indicate that it does, while others say there is no evidence to support such a conclusion. It is worth a try to see if it might work for you. If nothing else, it is a wonderful way to relieve stress, reduce anger or agitation and calm the mind.

- Breathe in through your nose slowly and deeply to the count of 4.
- Imagine breathing in peace and calm.
- Hold for the count of 4 as you take a moment.
- Then exhale through your mouth to the count of 4.
- Feel all of the tension and anxiety flow out of you as you let the breath go.
- Hold for the count of 4 as you take another moment. Repeat the square of 4 a further 8 times.

When you breathe make sure that you're using your tummy it should rise and fall. To check this put a hand on your tummy just above your belly button. It can help to imagine a square being drawn in your mind's eye; each breath is a side of the square. You will need to cycle around this process between 6 to 9 times to get the effect.

☐ Tick when done ✓

Action: Give it a go next time you feel pain, see how you feel less pain.

Distract yourself

Finding something to distract you is a great way of moving your attention away from the pain. The more and deeper you become involved in an activity the better. The more you are engaging with life (being in the now) then the less attention you pay to the pain.

Throw yourself 100% into it. It should be enjoyable, something you can become immersed in. It should be interesting, stimulating and holds your complete attention.

- Read a book
- Watch a good film or TV show
- Draw or paint
- Play some music
- Make something
- Do a crossword or sudoku
- Get a colouring book
- Build a model
- Clear out a drawer
- Wash your face/hands or brush your teeth
- Talk to a friend
- Play solitaire on your phone
- Play with a tangle, fidget cube, pin art
- Apply body lotion all over
- Take a nap

☐ Tick when done ✓
Action: Take a few moments and write some of your ideas beside this list of distractions. When you are in pain you can come back and work through them to see which ones work best for you.

Soak in a warm bath or take a shower
Warmth is a great way to reduce pain, tension and discomfort. It soothes tired, aching muscles and gives you a chance to unwind.

You can add 2-3 cups of Epsom salt. It's believed that magnesium helps to reduce swelling. It's something that helps to combat inflammation. You don't need the bath too hot; just warm enough for you to relax and be comfortable. Ensure that you are well hydrated as believe it or not you do sweat underwater.

If you have difficulty getting in and out of the bath then a warm shower can work wonders too. Just let the warm water flow over you and wash the old pain away.

☐ Tick when done ✓
Action: Take a bath or shower with the mindset of washing and easing away any pain or discomfort.

Laugh your heart out (not literally!)
Okay, this one might not be helpful soon after surgery as you will need time for you wounds to heal. Sneezing, coughing and laughing will be difficult for a while but will ease with time.

Laughter is a natural pain reliever. It boosts endorphins, those feel-good chemicals in your brain, and reduces stress hormones that can worsen pain.

Find a funny movie, call up a friend who cracks you up, or watch silly animal videos online. Even a forced chuckle can trick your body into a more relaxed state. Remember, laughter is the best medicine, and it's definitely a prescription you can fill yourself!

☐ Tick when done ✓
Action: Find something or someone that makes you laugh. Try Netflix or YouTube or download Finding Laughter that is a curated list of 94 movies, tv-series, books and songs will put a smile on your face. of www.myheartandmind.co.uk/bookBTB

Channel your inner artist
Doodling, colouring, or scribbling – any creative outlet can be a powerful distraction from pain. When your focus shifts to creating something beautiful, the discomfort takes a backseat. Plus, there's a sense of accomplishment that comes with finishing a project which is a great mood booster.

Maybe you working out your frustration with scribbling can help you vent and take your mind away from your body.

☐ Tick when done ✓

Action: Grab some crayons, put on some music, and let your creativity flow!

What are you saying about your pain?

In the chapter about anxiety, I asked *"Who are you talking to and what are you saying?"* The same thing applies here about pain.

How many times do you comment to yourself about your pain?

Begin to notice your thoughts around the pain or discomfort. Do you have thoughts about your pain even when you are not in pain? Are they positive or negative?

Are you saying to yourself things like: "I can't cope", "it will never stop", "oh I feel okay now but know sure as hell it will be back soon", "I'm always in pain" or "this pain is unbearable"?

If so, this is increasing your pain and discomfort, it's adding to a vicious circle of tension and pain. Your focus is on the problem and you are creating fear within your mind as you will be releasing cortisol and adrenaline that will be getting you up tight and ready to take action. Holding your body tight is not ideal for alleviating pain.

Do you have a story about your pain? Do you tell everyone you can how bad your pain is, and how it is constant and never goes away? Do you find yourself telling others or yourself the story of your last flare up?

Listen to yourself in conversations, yes, it is perfectly okay to talk about how you're feeling but try to use phrases that include hopeful words, the belief that the pain will subside, that it's not as bad as it once was. If you're not currently in pain or discomfort try not to mention it at all.

As you become aware of your thoughts start to use positive phrases such as: "I've got through this before and I can do it again", "this will pass as everything changes", "I give myself permission to heal", "this too shall pass", "I am resilient", "I am safe", "I am thankful for healing" or "I am whole, healthy and complete".

☐ Tick when done ✓

Action: Make yourself a list of phrases you can say even when you are in pain.

Essential oils

Aromatherapy is the ancient use of aromatic oils for improving your psychological or physical well-being.

It's used as a complementary therapy alongside standard pain relief treatment. The oils contain anti-inflammatory, analgesic and relaxing properties. They can be beneficial when inhaled or when used in massage. Some of the more useful oils that can help with pain relief are:

Bergamot oil
Peppermint oil
Rose oil
Rosemary oil
Sandalwood oil

Do not massage the oils directly onto your skin, they must be diluted with a carrier oil first. That said you can find them already made up for use.

You can burn incense, melts or candles. You could also sprinkle a few drops of oil on a cushion/pillow or use a hot stone/oil burner.

☐ Tick when done ✓
Action: If you don't already have any of these essential oils, ask your friends and family as they may be able to lend you some so you can give them a go.

Let it go ... A pain & discomfort reframe
This is another exercise where you are going to need to read through the technique a few times so you can remember and become familiar with the process. It's okay to read it as you go along but it sure helps if you have a sense of what is coming next.

Try this letting go exercise. This activity can be done with your eyes open or closed. As you follow through the steps of this activity in your mind's eye use a soothing gentle tone of voice to describe what you see, hear and feel in your imagination.

Do you know what I mean about your mind's eye? If you are not sure then just close your eyes and imagine your front door. What colour is it? Which side has the lock and handle? Do you have a knocker or a bell? What does it sound like? More than likely, you will have seen images of your front door and may have heard the bell or knocker. This is using your imagining in your mind's eye.

- Make yourself comfortable, in a quiet space. You can be sitting up or lying down and take a few relaxing deep breaths.

- Take a moment to notice where you feel the pain or discomfort. Where is it specifically in your body?

- In as much detail as you can describe to yourself what you imagine the pain would look, sound and feel like if it did have those attributes.

For example: What size is it? How wide? Long? How deep is it? What shape is it? What colour is the shape? Does it have a rough or smooth surface? Is it hot, warm or cool? Is it hard or soft? Is it giving off a sound, high pitch or low hum or maybe it is silent?

- Now imagine pushing and moving that shape out from within your body. Move the image you've created in front of you so it's floating in space and you can see it easily.

- Take some time to examine the shape and find out more about it. What happens when you move it around? If you make it bigger? Make it smaller? What happens when you make it vibrate?

- When you feel you know all there is to know, right now, ask your shape some questions such as: What do you really represent? What message do you have? What do you need?

- Pay attention to any answers and any thoughts that come into your mind. You might learn something interesting.

- Then confirm with yourself that you are you ready to let this shape go. If you have any doubts, come to mind then ask yourself: What needs to happen for me to let that shape go now?

- Next, you can begin to make some changes to that shape.

- What would be a soothing colour? Change the colour of the shape. What is a more comfortable shape? Change the shape and find the one that feels better. Make it smaller or bigger, which size improves the feeling the most? Move it closer or further away, again choose the position that creates the better feeling. Try moving it around if it is static, swinging gently in front of you perhaps. Warm it or cool it, play around with the sound or quiet it makes.

- After you have changed enough of the elements to feel good about that old shape, imagine that shape dissolving in front of you. Perhaps evaporating away, maybe jetting off into space, and potentially disappearing as magic dust. It could get larger and larger, thinner and thinner until it disappears from sight. Just let it go in any way that seems the most appropriate for you.

- Then take a couple more deep relaxing breaths and notice the tension has let go and how much better you are feeling now.

□□□□□□□□□ Tick when each time you use it ✓
Action: Try using this technique on 9 occasions when you are in pain and notice how it dissipates easily and effortlessly.

Visualise your victory lap
This one's my personal favourite. Close your eyes and imagine yourself completely healed, walking with ease, pain-free and strong. Picture yourself doing the activities you love, free from any limitations. Just spend a few moments each day doing this. This positive visualisation helps rewire your brain for success, reminding you of your goal and the strength you possess to achieve it. Practice this technique every day for a fortnight.

□□□□□□□□□□□□□□ Tick when done ✓
Action: For 14 days visualise yourself completely healed, pain free and doing the things you love without limitations.

Journaling for chronic pain
The most important person in any pain management intervention is you! It will help you keep records that can help you communicate effectively with your doctor. You can use the information you collect to learn about potential causes and changes you need to make. It's a fabulous tool to share with your doctor and it will give them an insight of what you are going through, it will help them manage your pain and discomfort.

Pain can be overwhelming. Keeping a pain journal is a great way for you to notice the frequency and the degree of pain that you experience. It helps you identify any triggers such as activities, feelings, emotions or even lack of activity.

It will highlight the patterns such as what pain relief medication has the best result. Which of the alternative therapies help. Is pain worse after certain foods and what activities are most beneficial?

Ideally make 3 entries per day, morning, and noon then again at bedtime. Avoid making an entry at the specific time of a flare-up, keep to a regular routine.

Decide how long you are going to complete your journal, perhaps a week or more. Complete them every day. Make no comparison or any judgement until you have completed your chosen period of time.

An added benefit to help with pain relief is to express your emotions, too. Write about how you feel and let it out in the form of a journal. It will help you identify the thoughts that keep you stuck in pain. You can then look to change them into more healing and helpful positive thoughts.

Keeping a journal will help you to notice the good and the bad days. It will highlight trends throughout the day and record what makes a difference to you. It can help change how you feel about that pain.

Your journal should include:

The day and time. The type of activities you have been doing since the last entry. The number of times you have felt pain or discomfort, where you felt it and how long it lasted.

Measure how intense the pain was, on a scale of 1 to 10? (1 = no pain and 10 = the worst pain imaginable). This will enable you to give the day an overall pain rating. For example: If you make 3 entries a day, add up the numbers and divide by 3 to give an overall pain rating for the day.

It's a good idea to also note what you have eaten or drank since the last entry, and if you took any medications to ease the pain, if so, did they give you relief. Did you try other ways to ease the pain including any therapies or techniques and if they helped you? Plus keep a note of any actions that gave you relief like standing, lying down or walking around.

☐☐☐☐☐☐☐ Tick when done ✓
Action: It is most beneficial for your medical team if you keep a journal for around 7 days if you are experiencing chronic pain. It helps them, like it does you see patterns and links so hopefully you get long-term relief.

If you think a pain journal would help you, you can download a FREE printable template file here www.myheartandmind.co.uk/bookBTB

Restoring Your Sleep

"Sleep is like a cat: It only comes to you if you ignore it." Gillian Flynn

Get ready to embark on a journey to reclaim one of life's most precious treasures – a good night's sleep. In the aftermath of a heart attack or heart surgery, sleep can be as elusive as a shooting star. I've been there, tossing and turning, and I get it. So, let's talk about why sleep matters post-cardiac events, why it can be challenging, and how you can regain the peaceful slumber you deserve.

Sleep is important it's not just a luxury, sleep is a lifeline for your overall well-being. Its absence doesn't just leave you groggy and irritable – it can escalate health risks, including the likelihood of another heart attack. Lack of sleep increases stress, triggers anxiety, fuels diabetes, and even contributes to calcium buildup in your heart arteries. The magic numbers? Around seven to nine hours of sleep a night. Your body and heart crave it.

Why is sleep so crucial? It's the reset button for your body and mind. Seven to eight hours of sleep (up to 9½ if you're a teen) gives your brain a chance to recharge, clears waste, and supports learning and memory. Your body cells repair and release hormones necessary for overall health and vitality. Consistent poor sleep? It's a triple threat – impairing productivity, memory, and concentration during your waking hours.

Ever wonder why your sleep patterns seem to play a hide-and-seek game with you? Here's the lowdown – sleep is essential for mood regulation. Your sleep cycle includes slow wave and rapid eye movement (REM) stages. If you've been feeling low or anxious, your REM periods might elongate, reducing the healing slow wave sleep. Translation: increased susceptibility to colds, feeling run down, and waking up exhausted.

I had personal struggles with sleep, pre-heart attack, I slept like a baby. The post-hospital period? It was a different story. Initially, all I could do was sleep – a vital part of the healing process. But, as the days marched on, the sandman decided to play hard to get. Falling asleep became a challenge, and waking up in the dead of night became an unwelcome routine.

Sleepless nights and the mind-body connection. Why is sleep suddenly a fickle friend post-cardiac event? It's not just about counting sheep. Physically, your body is in repair mode, and the energy demand is high. General anaesthesia's lingering effects can mess with your sleep patterns too. Add in the emotional and mental toll of the experience – the worry, the list-making, the contemplation of the next day – and you've got a recipe for restless nights.

What is insomnia? Have you ever found yourself lying in bed, wide awake, despite sheer exhaustion? Welcome to the world of insomnia. There are two types: primary, with no apparent cause, and secondary, linked to physical or psychological factors like medical conditions or grief. Short-term insomnia may last one to four weeks, while chronic insomnia can persist for over six weeks. Here's the kicker – it's more common than you think. About one in four people in the UK grapple with it at some point.

Mind over sleep matters and we can manage our minds and our thoughts. Do you have an active mind at bedtime? Ever found yourself in bed, eyes wide open, despite sheer exhaustion? You're not alone. This 'ping' moment of wakefulness can become a nightly ordeal, leaving you tossing, turning, and questioning your ability to sleep. The result? Mornings where you wake up feeling as if sleep has taken a vacation.

So, how do you quieten the mind chatter, ushering in the serenity needed for a restful night? The following insights and strategies will guide you towards better sleep. We're in this together, navigating the challenges and celebrating the victories on the road to peaceful slumber.

We'll dive into lifestyle and environment adjustments, explore body-centric approaches, tackle the midnight wake-up dilemma, and address fatigue despite sufficient sleep. Each step is a stride toward reclaiming the rejuvenating power of sleep.

Remember, my fellow heart warrior, the journey might be challenging, but the reward – a restful night's sleep – is worth every effort. As we unravel the mysteries of sleep, let's pave the way to a calmer, more relaxed life, where every night is an opportunity to dream, heal, and wake up refreshed. Let the sleep revolution begin!

Try not to do everything at once as you won't know what worked and what didn't. Go through it all and make a list of what you 'feel' might work for you. Also, note that it's not always a quick fix some things take repetition or practice. A new habit takes around 42 days to create, although sometimes much quicker.

Beyond the basics. Now that we've laid the groundwork for understanding the importance of sleep and the challenges we face post-cardiac event, let's dive into a treasure trove of strategies and remedies that can guide you towards peaceful slumber. Sleep is not just a luxury; it's a lifeline for your well-being. While my journey through post-heart attack sleep struggles opened my eyes to various solutions, remember, I'm not a doctor. Always consult with your doctor before trying any new remedies.

Consistent sleep/wake cycle

Your body loves routine, and your sleep/wake cycle is your best friend. Going to bed and waking up at the same time every day may sound simple, but it's a game-changer. Consistency is the secret to feeling refreshed and energised. But hey, life happens, and routines can be disrupted. If you need to tweak your bedtime, do it gradually, making 15-minute adjustments daily until you find your sweet spot.

Ever found yourself dozing off in front of the TV before bedtime? It happens to the best of us. Instead of succumbing to the sofa's lull, shake things up. Move around, and engage in mildly stimulating activities to prevent falling asleep prematurely. Trust me; it makes a world of difference.

Create a sleep-friendly environment

Your bedroom is your sleep haven, and its ambience can make or break your sleep quality. A few tweaks can transform it into a sleep sanctuary. Keep it dark, quiet, and cool – the trifecta for a blissful night's sleep. Surprisingly, a slightly cool room with proper ventilation is a sleep magnet. Invest in a comfortable mattress and pillows that cradle you in sleep-inducing comfort.

Technology-free zone

Repeat after me: no TV, no Netflix, and certainly no office gadgets in the bedroom! This space is reserved for sleep and, well, maybe a bit of intimacy. Having electronic gadgets in your bedroom tempts you to engage with them, leading to a stimulated mind, is not ideal for a restful night. Studies have shown that the blue light emitted by screens interferes with melatonin production – the hormone that signals bedtime to your brain. Avoid technology at least 30-60 minutes before bedtime. Consider an old fashioned alarm clock instead of using your phone. If you really can't live without it in the bedroom make sure you silence those notifications, and turn the phone face down beside your bed.

Pre-bedtime organisation ritual

Eliminate the stress of tomorrow by getting everything organised tonight. Knowing you've got it all sorted brings a sense of calm and readiness for a restful night ahead.

Sensual pre-sleep rituals

Treat yourself to a warm bath infused with lavender oil or a shower using lavender-scented body wash. The slightly warmer water will make your room feel cooler, while the lavender soothes your senses, paving the way for a serene bedtime.

Essential oils and herbs to optimise your sleep

I've mentioned herbs before, for aiding sleep try lavender and chamomile. Chamomile, especially as a drink or in oil form. It is one of the best herbs for reducing stress and promoting relaxation and sleep. You can find chamomile tea in many supermarkets, chemists and health food shops. Lavender oil is another that is well known to aid sleep and relaxation. You can put a few drops on a pillow or in an oil burner.

Try having a cup of chamomile tea and a warm bath about 1 hour before bed. Take about 20 drops of diluted lavender oil, and rub it over your body. Then get into a bath with Epsom salts (they contain magnesium that helps with sleep too). Relax for about 20 minutes then continue with the rest of your bedtime routine.

Mental rehearsal for tomorrow

As you nestle into bed, take a mental stroll through tomorrow. Visualise everything unfolding smoothly, just the way you'd like it to be. It's a subtle way to prep your mind for a peaceful night.

Capture thoughts in a notebook

Introduce a beautiful notebook and a pen you love to your bedside. Before bedtime, jot down any lingering thoughts, actions, or ideas for the next day. Clearing your mind's clutter creates the mental space you need to drift into a tranquil slumber. You can use it if you wake up and think that you are worrying that you may forget by morning.

Designated 'worry time'

If you're prone to bedtime worries – and who isn't? – here's a game-changer. Allocate yourself 10 minutes of 'worry time' earlier in the evening, well before bedtime. Decide that during this time, you'll allow yourself to worry. Set a timer and during this period of time you can think through all your worries and concerns, and then consciously let it go until the next day. It's a simple yet effective way to compartmentalise your worries.

Herbal remedies: Nature's lullabies

Ever considered the power of herbal remedies? Valerian, passionflower, hops, lavender, lemon balm, and Jamaican dogwood are commonly touted as insomnia soothers. While their benefits might lack a stamp of approval from medical trials, many swear by their calming effects.

Before you dive into the world of herbs, have a heart-to-heart with your doctor, pharmacist, and herbalist, especially if you're on other medications.

I first came across Valerian when I started menopause. It was recommended by my doctor instead of Hormone Replacement Therapy (HRT). I found it very effective in helping me go to sleep, stay asleep and sleep longer. Valerian is a herb and is classed as a supplement. There isn't enough research and studies at present to be definitive about how effective it is. Nor is there much known about how much is the optimum dose. This is something that you might want to try out for yourself. Always check with your doctor, pharmacist or herbalist especially if you are taking other medication. *Note:* It does have an unpleasant smell to me but one of my cats absolutely adores it, even more than catnip!

Prescribed sleep medication: Navigating the options

Considering sleeping tablets? Not all medications are cut from the same cloth. Each comes with its unique workings and potential side effects. Before making a decision, here are key questions to ask your doctor:

- How long do they last for?
- How long does it take for the sleeping pill to take effect?
- What's the risk of physical or psychological addiction?

Remember, prescribed sleep meds offer temporary relief, not a cure. Use them as a last resort, and only on an as-needed basis. Always speak to your primary care doctor first.

Non-prescription medicines: supermarket solutions
Venturing into over-the-counter remedies? They're readily available but watch out for that sneaky antihistamine hiding in many tablets.

Always check in with your doctor or pharmacist, as these seemingly harmless options may have hidden side effects and interactions with other medications that you are currently taking to protect your heart.

Melatonin: the sleep-wake regulator
Melatonin, a natural sleep hormone, could be your ally. Available over the counter too, it regulates your sleep-wake cycle. While it might not be a universal fix, it's worth exploring, especially if you're a night owl. Again, always check with your pharmacist first.

Lifestyle tweaks: caffeine, alcohol, and hydration
Are your caffeine habits interfering with your sleep? Swap to decaf and limit caffeine intake to mornings only. Bid adieu to alcohol too; it might make you sleepy initially, but it's a nighttime stimulant. Stay hydrated, but find that perfect balance. Too much may lead to nocturnal bathroom trips.

Whilst you may be using caffeine to keep you awake during the day it can be affecting how well you sleep. It can also cause palpitations. Make the change to decaffeinated coffee, tea and fizzy drinks.

If you quit completely, you may find you have a headache for a couple of days but this will soon pass. If you find it difficult to cut caffeine out of your diet completely then do reduce your consumption. Only having drinks with caffeine in the morning before noon. Stay clear of caffeine tablets. Make sure you read the packets of painkillers. Some of them contain caffeine to enhance the effect of pain relief.

Physical activity: A sleep elixir

Exercise, even light stretching, can be your sleep elixir. When you have finished cardio rehab or have been given the okay to exercise make sure you engage in regular cardio, but avoid vigorous workouts right before bedtime. Move your body; it will thank you with better sleep.

Nutrition

Where possible opt for light evening meals, easy on the digestion. Cut down on sugar and salt. Embrace tryptophan-rich foods like chicken, turkey, tuna, soya beans, and salmon, paired with carbohydrates. Integrate thiamine (vitamin B1) and magnesium into your diet – crucial for combating sleep disorders. Whole grains, nuts, and green leafy veggies are your allies.

Evaluating your beliefs about sleep

First and foremost, let's check your belief system. Are you convinced that you're sleep-deprived just because you aren't clocking in a solid eight hours like the mythical sleep perfectionist Margaret Thatcher? Remember, as we age, our sleep needs may evolve. If you're functioning well during the day, maybe, just maybe, you're getting enough sleep. Imagine the freedom of ditching the worry about those eight hours and relishing the extra moments you have in the day. A sleep journal can really help identify what's going on for you.

Breathe your way to sleep

Enter the world of deep breathing – a quick ticket to relaxation. These exercises aren't just for yogis; they're your secret weapon against stress and anxiety. As you are lying in bed, ready to ease into a peaceful slumber here's a simple breathing routine to guide you:

1. Get comfortable.
2. Place one hand on your chest and the other on your tummy.
3. Inhale deeply for about 7 seconds – let the hand on your tummy rise while the chest remains relatively still.
4. Hold your breath for 3 seconds.

5. Exhale slowly for approximately 11 seconds.
6. Allowing the tummy to fall.

Feel free to continue focusing on your breath for 12 cycles and then allow yourself to find your own natural rhythm.

If you're feeling proactive, run through this exercise once a day while sitting in a chair for 12 breath cycles. It's a small investment with a big return – a more relaxed mind and a smoother transition into sleep. It will teach your mind and body how to relax.

Note: The numbers given for the breath lengths are only suggestions. Only do what you have been told you can do or that is comfortable for you. The important bit is that the outbreath (exhalation) is longer than the inhaled breath.

The art of self-soothing

Picture this: a day filled with relaxation, leading to a night of uninterrupted sleep. It's not wishful thinking; it's the power of self-soothing. Throughout the day, practice the art of saying 'Stop, relax, soften' when stress creeps in. Drop those shoulders, release the jaw, take deep breaths – you can do this anywhere, anytime. Pair it with a mental vacation to a pleasant place or memory, and watch how swiftly you can calm yourself.

Breaking the cycle of worry

Ever found yourself lying in bed, dreading the hours of sleeplessness ahead? It's time to break the cycle of worrying about not sleeping and challenge those negative thoughts. Imagine this:

a) Situation: Lying awake in bed
b) Thoughts: I'll never sleep, I'll be exhausted in the morning, I won't have any energy, I can't cope, I'm going to be miserable tomorrow
c) Outcome: More worry, longer wakefulness

Sound familiar? It's time to replace those thoughts with more sleep-friendly alternatives:

a) Situation: Lying awake in bed
b) Thoughts: I can't sleep, I'll get up and make some warm milk, I'll engage in a calming activity, I'll go back to bed soon, I'll try a relaxation technique. Even if I don't sleep, I know I can manage – I've done it before
c) Outcome: More sleep.

Future visualisation for a restful tomorrow

Harness the power of future visualisation while comfortably lying in bed. In your imagination run through your next day or a future event, savouring every detail – the colours, sounds, feelings, and even the smells. Imagine everything unfolding really slowly and perfectly. This mental rehearsal sets the stage for a night of tranquil sleep.

Soothing background sounds

Bring the sounds of nature, rain, ocean waves, or a distant thunderstorm into your sleep sanctuary. These background noises, available online, signal to your brain that all is well, minimising the chances of startling awake.

If you go for music, choose something soft and slow-paced, ensuring it won't unexpectedly switch to an upbeat tempo.

Be cautious with mobile devices, though; the blue light and notifications can disrupt your sleep.

Talking to yourself and others

Sometimes the cause of insomnia can be because you are worried about having poor sleep. A vicious circle. Do you tell yourself that you won't sleep? Do you find yourself telling others that you won't sleep? Do you lay in bed worrying about not being able to sleep the moment you're in bed?

If this is the case it can be your belief about the lack of sleep that is the problem and keeping you awake. Change it up. Begin by noticing what you are saying. Practice changing your thoughts and tell yourself you can sleep. That you will sleep easily and effortlessly. You'll be surprised at how this simple thing can make a huge difference.

Guided relaxation and meditation

Unlock the power of guided relaxation and meditation. Whether it's progressive muscle relaxation, guided imagery, self-hypnosis, or deep breathing exercises, having a guide can make the journey more seamless. Download a guided relaxation recording or explore meditation apps like Headspace. Incorporating these practices into your routine can contribute to pain management, stress reduction, and improved sleep quality.

Teaching yourself, your mind and your body how to relax can be practised during the day. This helps you learn so that at night when you close your eyes and relax it comes easy for you.

You can download a FREE 20-minute Guided Relaxation file here
www.myheartandmind.co.uk/bookBTB

Hypnotherapy for deep, restful sleep

Sometimes, insomnia lingers, even after the stress has eased. Hypnotherapy offers a path to reprogram your mind for restful sleep. Whether it's stress, anxiety, or an ingrained habit of sleeplessness, hypnosis aims to communicate with your unconscious mind, instigating positive changes. Sessions with a therapist can uncover the root cause and initiate personalised changes. Self-hypnosis techniques learned during therapy can be a valuable tool for maintaining control over your sleep patterns.

Talk yourself to sleep

So, it's time for bed, and you're nicely snuggled up and ready to fall asleep and yet it alludes you. Give this a go and engage in bedtime conversations with yourself using either of these creative techniques:

a) Using the Alphabet: Start at A, finding items that begin with each letter sequentially. Reverse the process from Z to A if you reach the end. Think animals, product names, names (boys and girls), or even elements from the periodic table.

b) Affirmations: Embrace the power of positive affirmations, repeating them as if they've already happened. Affirmations like 'I am happy and content,' 'I am in total control of my thoughts,' or 'I enjoy natural sleep every night' can create a soothing mental environment conducive to sleep.

In this chapter, we've covered an array of options to enhance your sleep quality and there's a chance you're thinking what no tick boxes. Ahaa, I thought I would wait until the end as remember, these are tools, not one-size-fits-all solutions. Consult your healthcare team, listen to your body, and let's embark on this journey together. Sleep well, my fellow heart warriors – your journey to restful nights awaits.

Download my sleep easy checklist

As there are so many activities more than I have included in this chapter. I have created a FREE separate printable download of a checklist containing a total of 53 tips to help you sleep easy. www.myheartandmind.co.uk/bookBTB.

☐ Tick when done ✓

Action: Work through them and it will help you keep track of what you tried. Also mark if it the tips worked or not so you can build your own sleep toolkit. Please remember that some techniques need to be practised several times so you get the cumulative effect of the process.

Love, Sex, and Intimacy

"Passion is the quickest to develop, and the quickest to fade. Intimacy develops more slowly, and commitment more gradually still."
Robert Sternberg

Okay, let's talk about the elephant in the room – or should I say, the elephant in your heart? Because after a heart attack or surgery, rediscovering the magic in your love life might feel like attempting a high-wire act without a safety net. But fear not, my friend, I'm here to spill the beans on reigniting the flames of passion after cardiac adventures.

Now, before we dive into the juicy details, let's get one thing straight – always, always follow your doctor's advice before engaging in any amorous escapades post-heart event. It's not a suggestion; it's a golden rule.

A frequent question that comes up is how soon can I rekindle my love life. Well, this entirely depends on the individuals but I have heard stories that it doesn't have to be very long at all. In the initial weeks post-hospital, you're in the rest zone.

It is always worth asking the when questions before you leave the hospital. But when the green light for intimacy flickers, there are a few checkpoints on the map.

If you don't have chest pain, shortness of breath or heart rhythm problems, you can usually resume sex after 1-2 weeks.

If you had open-heart surgery, you may be able to resume sex in about 6-8 weeks. It takes more time for the incision and breastbone to heal. You may need an exercise stress test to see if sexual activity is safe for you.

If you experience chest pain, shortness of breath or other heart symptoms during sexual activity, you should stop and notify your health care professional.

So, let's address the elephant's shadow – the common issues with sex and intimacy post-heart surgery. High blood pressure survivors might encounter erectile dysfunction, loss of libido, vaginal dryness, pain, or the elusive orgasm that seems to be playing hide and seek.

Does the mere thought of intimacy cause enough distress without even getting physical? It's a double whammy. But guess what? Communication is your knight in shining armour. Open up to your partner, doctor, friend, or family member. Sharing your thoughts is an intimate act in itself, fostering a deeper connection.

Some of the hiccups I've described might be due to the meds you're on or in my case taken off of, I loved my Hormone Replacement Therapy (HRT). A quick chat with your doctor or pharmacist can work wonders – they might tweak things around. And here's the truth bomb: your heart's well-being comes first, so take the meds you need. If erectile dysfunction is a hurdle, fear not; there are safe options available.

Feeling a bit dry down there? No worries – a little lube can work wonders. Don't be shy; remember, sex is excellent cardio and a hormonal booster.

Now, the million-dollar question – could sex cause another heart attack? It's a fair concern. Talk to your doctor, because recovery times vary. If you're in the clear, a bit of exercise in the sheets can be a heart-friendly bonus. No need for a marathon, a short sprint can do wonders for your recovery.

And let's not forget the body image blues. Surgery can leave scars, and your body may feel like a different landscape. But here's the truth: your partner loves all of you – inside and out. Scars fade, conditions improve, and age is just a number. Your self-esteem will make a comeback, trust me.

Not in the mood for the physical stuff yet? No sweat. Romance isn't dead. A candle-lit meal or a hand-holding stroll in the park can reignite the spark without diving into the deep end.

Communication is the key to intimacy. Start the conversation and embrace the nerves – they might just be the spark your nervous system needs. And don't forget the power of cuddling. Being close and holding each other is a love language in itself.

In the grand scheme of things, take your time. This is a monumental shift in your life, and navigating it will take time. Shower each other with love notes, share your feelings, and above all, cut yourselves some slack. The magic is still there, waiting to be rediscovered when you're ready.

How do you feel about sex are you ready?

☐ Tick when done ✓

Action: Take some time to consider how you feel about intimacy or self-gratification as some of you may be single. Are there any should do, must do or have to thoughts? You will know when you are ready.

Open communication

☐ Tick when done ✓

Action: Talk openly with your partner about your fears, desires, and expectations. If you feel pressure be honest, if you’re up to it bear in mind your partner may be fearful themselves. It's a journey you embark on together.

Go slow

☐ Tick when done ✓

Action: There's no need to rush. Take it slow, listen to your body, and find a pace that works for both of you.

Educate yourself

☐ Tick when done ✓

Action: Knowledge is power. Understand how medications may affect intimacy and explore potential solutions with your healthcare team.

Celebrate your body

☐ Tick when done ✓

Action: Embrace your scars and view them as a testament to your strength. Your body has weathered a storm and emerged resilient. Be proud of it.

Seek professional guidance

☐ Tick when done ✓

Action: If concerns persist, seek advice from healthcare professionals. They're here to help you navigate these challenges.

Get connected with other single people

☐ Tick when done ✓

Action: If you are single or lonely then come over and join the Heart-to-Heart Community for Singles Living with Heart Issues. Join and make friends over at www.facebook.com/groups/hearties2hearties.

Shadows of the Heart - Cardiophobia

"Nothing in life is to be feared. It is only to be understood." Marie Curie

It's entirely normal to experience anxiety, depression, fear, and anger after heart surgery, heart attacks, or the harrowing experience of cardiac arrest. However, in this exploration, we shine a spotlight on a phenomenon that goes beyond the expected emotional response - it's called cardiophobia.

So, why delve into the complexities of cardiophobia? Because knowledge is power. Understanding cardiophobia empowers you to recognise and navigate the intricate pathways of anxiety, fear, and uncertainty that may accompany the road to recovery.

Cardiophobia, also known as the fear of heart disease or heart-related events, is a psychological condition that can affect individuals who have had cardiac issues. It's not just about the heart; it's about unscrambling the fears that entwine with it. Traumatic experiences, fear of the unknown, post-traumatic stress disorder (PTSD), health anxiety, and a sense of loss of control can contribute to the development of cardiophobia.

Experiencing a heart event is traumatic, and cardiophobia can be an intense fear of heart-related problems, particularly another attack. Symptoms often mimic those of a heart attack, leading to the fight-or-flight response. Chest tightness, palpitations, shortness of breath, and a sense of impending doom become part of the emotional landscape.

Understanding the physiological connection is crucial. Anxiety amplifies normal bodily sensations, and individuals with cardiophobia may misinterpret harmless sensations, reinforcing the fear. Studies suggest that 10-20% of individuals experience significant anxiety post-cardiac events, impacting quality of life and leading to social isolation.

Cardiophobia is characterised by an intense fear of heart problems and potential heart attack and is classified as a "specific phobia" within the Diagnostic and Statistical Manual of Mental Disorders, Fifth Edition, Text Revision (DSM-5-TR), falling under the umbrella of anxiety disorders.

- Intense fear or anxiety: This intense fear specifically targets the possibility of having a heart problem, often exceeding the actual risk.
- Disproportionate response: The level of fear and anxiety experienced is significantly greater than the actual danger of having a heart attack in the situation.
- Clinical significance: Fear and anxiety cause significant distress in daily life, impacting the individual's ability to function normally.
- Avoidance behaviour: Individuals with cardiophobia actively try to avoid situations they believe might trigger their symptoms.

Furthermore, cardiophobia can trigger panic attacks, sudden episodes of intense anxiety accompanied by various physical symptoms, including:

- Sweating
- Shaking

- Shortness of breath
- Rapid heartbeat
- Chest pain or tightness
- Numbness or tingling sensations
- Dizziness
- Feeling faint

It's important to note that while some of these physical symptoms may overlap with actual heart problems, cardiophobia is a mental health condition, and these symptoms are primarily due to anxiety and not indicative of an underlying physical issue.

But how can you tell the difference? It's not easy and my saying "if in doubt check it out" stands true. The overlap between physical sensations of anxiety and potential heart problems can create a significant source of distress for individuals. This can trigger a vicious cycle where increased anxiety leads to physical symptoms like rapid heartbeat and chest tightness, which then intensify the fear of experiencing a heart attack. This loop can be particularly difficult to manage as distinguishing between anxiety-induced symptoms and those of an actual heart condition often proves challenging without undergoing medical evaluation. Consulting a healthcare professional is crucial to differentiate between the two and receive appropriate care.

The good news is cardiophobia is treatable. Various techniques and therapies can help you manage and overcome this fear. Cognitive-behavioural therapy (CBT), exposure therapy, mindfulness, relaxation techniques, biofeedback, graded exercise therapy, education, support groups, medication, and hypnotherapy are among the strategies that can be tailored to individual needs.

Here are some self-help strategies to ease the symptoms of cardiophobia:

Understanding the normalcy of sensations

☐ Tick when done ✓

Action: Educate yourself about the normal sensations and changes in the body that may occur post-cardiac events. Knowing what is expected can help distinguish between typical bodily experiences and irrational fears.

Accurate information

☐ Tick when done ✓

Action: Seek accurate information about your cardiac health, the recovery process, and the likelihood of future events. This knowledge can counteract misconceptions and provide a more realistic perspective.

Mindful breathing

☐☐☐☐☐☐☐☐☐ Tick when done ✓

Action: Practice mindfulness and deep breathing exercises to stay present and calm. Focus on your breath, inhaling slowly and deeply, and exhaling with intention. This can help reduce overall anxiety and create a sense of calm. Try this 9 times in situations that have previously felt impossible.

Stay in the now, this MOMENT

Try this 5-4-3-2-1 Grounding exercise. A technique you can use at any time, any place or any situation.

1. Notice FIVE things you see around you. Maybe it's your pet, a tree, perhaps a pen, the door, a mug or maybe it is a spot on the ceiling, no matter what, state 5 things you see.
2. Notice FOUR things you can touch. It could be your hair, hands, ground, grass, pillow, desk, phone etc, whatever it may be, list out the 4 things you can feel.
3. Acknowledge THREE things you can hear. This needs to be external to your thoughts, do not focus on your inner chatter; possibly you can hear a clock, the wind, laughter, a car, or a

dog barking. What is audible to you at the moment is what you list.

4. Become aware of TWO things you can smell. If you can't easily find something go find something. Walk around and start to sniff something out. You could go to your bathroom to smell soap, your kitchen or outside to smell anything in nature, or even could be as simple as smelling your sofa or your clothes. Whatever it may be, take in the smells around you.
5. Become mindful of ONE thing you can taste. What does the inside of your mouth taste like, gum, tea or coffee, your fingers or your pen? Focus on your mouth and tongue and notice what you can taste.

Going through these steps will help ground you in present thinking, they bring me back to the MOMENT every time.

□□□□□□□□□ Tick when done ✓
Action: When you are next in a situation that you think, you can't handle use this technique. Try it on 9 different difficult situations.

Progressive muscle relaxation (PMR)
Engage in PMR to systematically tense and relax different muscle groups. This technique promotes relaxation and reduces muscle tension associated with anxiety. If you have difficulty sleeping this is a great technique and you can use it sequentially to help you drift off to sleep.

1. Become aware of your breathing. Breathing easily.
2. Become aware of your toes. Tense them then let them relax.
3. Become aware of your feet. Flex them and then let them relax.
4. Become aware of your calves. Tense them and then let them relax.
5. Become aware of your knees. Tense them and then let them relax. Becoming more relaxed.
6. Become aware of your thighs. Tense them and then let them relax.

7. Become aware of your stomach. Pull it in and then relax it.
8. Become aware of your bottom. Tense it and let it relax. More and more relaxed.
9. Become aware of your back. Tense it and let it relax.
10. Become aware of your chest. Let it relax, relaxing now.
11. Become aware of your upper arms. Tense them and let them relax.
12. Become aware of your hands, flex them and let them relax. Drifting away.
13. Become aware of your shoulders. Tense them and let them relax.
14. Become aware of your jaw. Clench your teeth and then allow them to open a little.
15. Become aware of your cheeks. Imagine that they are being massaged to relax completely.
16. Become aware of your eyes. How heavy they are. Let the muscles around them relax.
17. Become aware of your forehead. Frown slightly and let your forehead relax.
18. Become aware of your scalp. Imagine someone massaging it restfully, massaging down the back of your neck, that lovely relaxed feeling.

☐☐☐☐☐☐ Tick when done ✓
Action: When you are next feeling tense, panicked, anxious, uptight or can't sleep, try this and give it ago on 6 separate occasions.

Challenge negative thoughts
Identify and challenge negative thoughts related to heart health. Ask yourself if these thoughts are based on evidence or if they are exaggerated fears. Replace irrational thoughts with more balanced and realistic ones.

This is where understanding the normalcy of your sensations and having accurate information will help immensely. Start to pay attention to your thoughts and feelings and start a list of the most common ones. These are the ones that you should get accurate information about and a full understanding of what are normal sensations. Once you have a list of your reoccurring thoughts you can write them in a journal and then write balanced and realistic evidence that you can refer to when you are feeling overwhelmed.

Negative thoughts	Balancing thoughts

Tick when done ✓ ☐
Action: Notice your regular alarming thoughts and write them in a journal.

Tick when done ✓ ☐
Action: Counter all of your negative thoughts with the facts that are balanced and realistic.

Incorporate relaxing activities
Include relaxing physical activities such as yoga or tai chi in your

routine. These practices not only promote physical fitness but also emphasise mindfulness and relaxation.

☐ Tick when done ✓
Action: Research what classes are available near you for when you are fit enough to take part. Maybe enlist a friend or loved one to join in with you.

Connect with other hearties

Join support groups or communities where individuals share similar experiences. Connecting with others who understand your journey can provide a sense of camaraderie and reduce feelings of isolation.

☐ Tick when done ✓
Action: Find out if there are any local in-person cardiac support groups and attend cardiac rehabilitation classes.

Open communication

Communicate openly with loved ones, friends and healthcare professionals and tell them about your fears and concerns. Discuss your symptoms, thoughts, and feelings so you can receive appropriate support and guidance.

☐ Tick when done ✓
Action: Share how you are feeling with healthcare professionals.

☐ Tick when done ✓
Action: Involve your loved ones and family tell them how you are feeling.

☐ Tick when done ✓
Action: Speak with your friends & colleagues.

Remember, these self-help strategies are meant to complement professional guidance, and it's essential to consult with healthcare providers for a comprehensive approach tailored to your individual needs. Consistency and patience are key as you incorporate these strategies into your daily life.

Embarking on the journey of understanding cardiophobia is not just about conquering shadows but embracing the light within. By recognizing the difference between expected emotional responses and cardiophobia, by understanding the science and symptoms you can navigate the intricate landscape of emotions post-cardiac events with resilience and hope. Remember, the heart is not just a muscle; it's a resilient warrior, and so are you.

Shadows of the Heart - Pumphead

"My brain is experiencing technical difficulties, please stand by." Unknow

Ah, the mysterious world of Postperfusion syndrome. It is also called pumphead – a term that gained popularity when patients started sharing their post-surgery experiences. The list of symptoms reads like a confusing puzzle: brain fog, confusion, headaches, dizziness, and double vision. It's like trying to navigate a foggy day without a compass. But here's the kicker – these symptoms seemed to be playing favourites, showing up more prominently in those who had undergone bypass surgery.

Now, let's unravel the mystery. Why does pumphead seem to have a soft spot for bypass patients? The initial hunch was that it had something to do with the perfusion machine – the gadget responsible for keeping blood and oxygen flowing during heart surgery. It made sense; teeny tiny blood clots forming on the brain due to the machine's use could lead to cognitive issues. Case closed, right? Not quite.

Recent studies threw a curveball. Bypass patients who skipped the perfusion machine still experienced pumphead symptoms.

I have even heard that people who have had stents also experience the symptoms of pumphead even though there wasn't any invasive heart surgery. Still the heart will have been interrupted or had a percutaneous coronary intervention.

So, it's not a one-machine show; any tinkering with the heart and aorta might be the culprit. Enter a dance of theories – blood pressure drops, body temperature fluctuations, and oxygen levels taking a dip, all potential suspects during heart surgery or a cardiac event.

And here we are, caught in the crossfire of debates. Why? Because the scientific community loves a good puzzle, and the brain is one intricate maze.

But let's bring it down to the real stuff – how do you know if pumphead is doing a little dance in your head? Feeling off-balance lately? Tripped over thin air, maybe? Is problem-solving suddenly feeling like solving advanced calculus? Perhaps confusion and brain fog are your uninvited guests. Throw in some depression, anxiety, or a personality shift, and you've got yourself a potential pumphead party.

Now, these symptoms might be post-surgery commoners, thanks to the anaesthesia and all, but if they're overstaying their welcome, it's time to summon the medical cavalry. The sooner, the better! Don't play the guessing game; let your doctor be the detective.

And here's the good news – pumphead isn't untameable, it is treatable. So, toss that shyness aside, and speak up. If in doubt, check it out. Consult your primary doctor, and maybe, venture into the realm of neurology. Your brain deserves a little TLC.

Remember, I've been on this rollercoaster of cardiac event surprises, and I get it, well some of it. It's like navigating uncharted waters, but you're not alone. Many have walked this path, stumbled upon pumphead, and emerged victorious. Speaking up is not a sign of weakness; it's a declaration of resilience. Take the reins of your health journey, and let pumphead take a backseat.

So, here's the battle cry – if pumphead is crashing your party, don't let it in for a permanent stay. Seek help, face it head-on, and let your recovery journey be one of triumph. You've got this!

Now that we've shed some light on this mysterious condition, let's talk about some activities that can play the role of bouncers, showing pumphead the exit door. These simple yet effective strategies might just be your pass to a clearer mind and a smoother recovery journey.

Mental gymnastics
Flex those cognitive muscles! Engage in activities that challenge your brain – puzzles, crosswords, or even learning a new skill. Think of it as a spa day for your brain, giving it the pampering it needs to bounce back from the post-surgery fog.

☐ Tick when done ✓
Action: Buy a book or download an app to your phone.

Physical exercise
It's not just about breaking a sweat; it's about boosting those endorphins. Exercise is a magical way of not only improving your physical health but also enhancing cognitive function. Whether it's a gentle stroll, yoga, or approved post-surgery workouts, get that body moving.

☐ Tick when done ✓
Action: When you are given the okay by your medical team, find an activity that you enjoy and where you can meet other people.

Mindful meditation
Picture this – a serene mental landscape where pumphead's chaos is replaced by tranquillity. Meditation isn't just a buzzword; it's a powerful tool. Even a few minutes a day can help calm the storm in your mind, promoting mental clarity and peace.

☐ Tick when done ✓
Next time you have a bathroom break, take a few moments and imagine your happy place. Close your eyes and take a breath, remember what you see, hear, feel, smell and taste in a place or time where you were calm and happy.

Adequate sleep
Sleep, the unsung hero of recovery. Ensure you're getting the recommended 7-8 hours of shut-eye. Quality sleep rejuvenates both body and mind. Create a cozy bedtime routine, dim the lights, and bid pumphead farewell for the night.

☐ Tick when done ✓
Action: Download and complete my Sleep Easy Check List available for download here www.myheartandmind.co.uk/bookBTB.

Balanced nutrition
Think of your brain as a high-performance car – it needs the right fuel. Go for a well-balanced diet rich in omega-3 fatty acids, antioxidants, and vitamins. Your brain will thank you, and pumphead might just pack its bags in the face of such nourishment.

☐ Tick when done ✓
Plan a few changes that can improve your mental health.

Social engagement
Don't underestimate the power of human connection. Engage with friends, family, or support groups. Sharing experiences, laughter, and even frustrations can be therapeutic. A strong support system can be a formidable ally against pumphead.

☐ Tick when done ✓
Action: I am going to say it again, you will always be welcome in the My Heart & Mind Community. Come over and get to know us.
www.facebook.com/groups/myheartandmindcommunity.

There are also many other Facebook groups specifically for people who are experiencing symptoms.

Remember, these activities aren't just strategies; they're your arsenal against post-cardiac hitches. Incorporate them into your daily routine, and watch their grip loosen.

Your recovery journey is a dynamic process, and these activities are your partners in progress. So, go ahead, take charge, and let pumphead know it's time to make way for clarity, vitality, and a renewed sense of well-being.

.

It's Time to Say 'Until Next Time'

As we draw the curtain on this journey, it's time to bid a temporary farewell – until the next time we meet and I hope we do. Not because of another event but because you have joined a group and become part of a community.

Being welcomed into your life has been a genuine honour, and the opportunity to share my thoughts with you has been immensely fulfilling.

Much like life itself, change is an ever-evolving process. In navigating new situations, remember that your adaptability is key. Seize each moment because life isn't a destination but a continuous journey.

Take note of the techniques that resonated most with you and integrate them into your daily life. Consider the measurable outcomes you aimed for – where do you stand now, and what's the next chapter you want to unfold?

While none of the activities I've introduced are groundbreaking on their own, their true power lies in their collective impact. When woven together, they have the potential to reshape your life in profound ways.

Remember, it's been your dedication, determination, and curiosity that fuelled this transformation. You took charge, exploring the possibilities of a different life.

The techniques we've explored are just the tip of the iceberg. If you've found success, know that there's room for even greater achievements. Your journey doesn't end here.

If this experience has resonated with you, consider paying it forward. Share this book with someone who might benefit – family, friends, your cardiologist, surgeon, nursing team, or colleagues.

You've proven time and again that transformation is within your grasp. Until we meet again on this journey, keep embracing change and forging your path toward a more fulfilling life.

Wishing you love, luck and laughter...

.

About The Author

Sallie Crawley has over 17 years of experience as a coach and therapist. She is a certified Life Coach and ILM Executive Coach and Mentor. She is also certified as a Master Practitioner of Neuro Linguistic Programming and trained as a Clinical Hypnotherapist.

Since overcoming breast cancer and surviving a heart attack, she specialises in helping people who have had a heart attack learn to live life and love life again. She helps with anxiety, panic, sleeplessness, creating the mindset to make exercise and dietary changes, relaxation, smoking cessation and confidence.

As a North Londoner, her career was originally in the print and communications industry. Spending some 16 years she gained experience working in commercial, report and accounts and food labelling printing companies. She managed teams in admin, production and sales.

After a year out to be a full-time mum and a move to a small village,

Sallie had a career change. In 2002 she joined the RSPB (conservation charity) and supported volunteering throughout the UK for 17 years. As the HQ Volunteering Operations Team Manager, she is inspired and proud of the contribution that the Charity's 12,000+ volunteers make to the cause.

Sallie also proudly volunteers as a Trustee of a local charity, the Hunts Cancer Community Network (HCCN). Empowering people to take control of their diagnosis and take an active part in managing their health. By providing services in the areas of education, wellbeing, exercise and nutrition. HCCN is helping to transform cancer care in the Huntingdonshire Community.

She lives in Cambridgeshire, UK with her daughter, their dog, two cats and a fish called Lonely.

Other Books on Amazon

Cognitive Cardio - Puzzles for a Healthy Heart & Mind. Pass the time, stimulate your brain, and learn more about your heart health during cardiac recovery through crosswords and puzzles.

UK https://amzn.to/3Lt3p7v
US www.amazon.com
AU www.amazon.com.au
CA www.amazon.ca

The Beat Goes On - Supporting you with the practical and emotional side of life when living with heart disease when you're first diagnosed.

UK https://amzn.to/4bwWgxz
US www.amazon.com
AU www.amazon.com.au
CA www.amazon.ca

Printed in Dunstable, United Kingdom

65737201R00087